Alexander McKenzie

Cambridge Sermons

Alexander McKenzie

Cambridge Sermons

ISBN/EAN: 9783337289911

Printed in Europe, USA, Canada, Australia, Japan

Cover: Foto ©Suzi / pixelio.de

More available books at **www.hansebooks.com**

CAMBRIDGE SERMONS

BY
ALEXANDER McKENZIE

BOSTON
D. LOTHROP AND COMPANY
32 FRANKLIN STREET

These sermons are, for the most part, printed from reports made by Mr. H. W. Gleason.

CONTENTS.

I.— The one Life	. . . . .	7
II.— Who loved Me	. . . .	31
III.— Choose whom ye will serve	. .	49
IV.— Looking toward the Sea	. .	70
V.— The good Merchant	. . .	83
VI.— Why stand ye gazing	. . .	102
VII.— Not by might, but by Spirit	. .	122
VIII.— Grieving the Holy Spirit	. .	142
IX.— Turning Northward	. . .	162
X.— What must I do	. . . .	183
XI.— The Love of God manifested	. .	183
XII.— We shall be like Him	. . .	222
XIII.— The unchanging Christ	. .	240
XIV.— The wayside Seed	. . . .	263
XV.— Truth commending Itself	. .	283
XVI.— The Power of an endless Life	.	303

CAMBRIDGE SERMONS.

I.

THE ONE LIFE.

SCRIPTURE LESSON: *Revelation*, *Chapter* xxii.
TEXT: And I, even I only, am left; and they seek my life, to take it away. — *I Kings*, xix: 10.

"I EVEN I only, am left." What a chance he had, the only man in Israel who loved God, and whom God approved! What a communion must have been given him as the Spirit of God dwelt with him! What an opportunity for usefulness! He was not bearing to the people a common thing; he was not standing as a witness to that which everybody knew, and offering to men that which others could give to them; he was the only man who could make the people see God; who was authorized to speak for him; to whom men might point and say, "Behold the servant of God." Our influence is so much curtailed, and our opportunities to bless the world, because there are so many others who have the same kind of goods to sell, the same kind of spirit to illustrate, the same sort of influence to exert, that when one finds himself standing alone, holding a great treasure, or representing some great truth, it is then that his opportunity has come. It sometimes happens that there is one only of a family who loves Christ. What an opportunity is his! There may be only one in a circle of friends who serves God; there may be only one in a class, one among the clerks in a store, one in a firm of merchants, one in any of the associations of life. Almost everybody we know may be a stranger to God. What a divine opportunity, to be promptly and heartily improved! It was a misconception on this man's part, that he was alone in his fidelity; yet the influence of seven thousand who had not bowed the knee to Baal, and whose lips had not kissed him, went for very little so long as they chose to be concealed. No one wishes to deny the value of secret piety; but no man ever read in his New Testament that secret piety was enough. It is not more plainly required of us that we believe on the Lord Jesus Christ, than that we let the world know that we believe on him. The word of the Gospel which we have read this morning, which bids whosoever will to come to him, with equal emphasis bids whosoever comes to repeat the word, that it may pass from man to man, and land to land, until, all through the earth, the other sheep which are not of this fold are brought into the one flock under the one shepherd.

Nobly had this man Elijah used his opportunity. When he was called upon to stand alone, he stood alone. "I, I only remain a prophet of the Lord; but Baal's prophets are four hundred and fifty men." He matched himself against them all; he denied nothing; he concealed nothing; he withheld nothing. He stood out in that simple personality, one man here and four hundred and fifty there; one man with God and the hundreds with Baal; and this one man with God outnumbered and subdued them all. Then there came that reaction which comes so often; a reaction which is needed. It is scarcely possible that with such success and such wonderful achievements as marked the life of Elijah, he should be able to bear this pressure and to live in this exalted state. It was almost inevitable that, when the excitement was withdrawn, when no longer there were hundreds of men to resist him, and he stood alone, the conqueror — it was almost inevitable that his heart should fail him. It was necessary that he should have this recalling to himself. God gives it to us; he gave it to Elijah; he gave it to St. Paul afterwards. Lest he should be exalted out of measure by the abundance of the revelation, lest he should be exalted in his own thoughts and be separated from his work, God gave to St. Paul a thorn in the flesh. He gave to Elijah that woman Jezebel to bring him to humility, that he might feel it was God alone who was great, even though he was the prophet of God. There was a falling back into dismay and disappointment; there was a halting, because of the fear which oppressed his soul. Then there came those grand lessons. One brought him down from the comfort of the proud seclusion in which he lived. He was reminded that there were seven thousand who were like himself; seven thousand faithful hearts. It was not altogether a pleasant thought for a man who was boasting himself in his peculiar goodness. As if that was not enough, he was reminded that it was not very essential that he should live; for there was a farmer's boy following the oxen along the plains of Abel-meholah, who would be ready to stand in his place and take up his work; so that for the world it mattered very little whether Elijah lived or not. How much there was to make this man find his place; not to take away anything which he had wrought or anything from his willingness to do, but to bring him to the level of other men, until he found in his own heart that which the Scripture has been frank enough to write concerning him, that "Elijah was a man subject to like passions as we are," so that he needed the same discipline that he might keep the faith. But Elijah lived, went to Beersheba, left his servant behind him, plunged into the wilderness and there laid him down in his despair and prayed that he might die. Then there came that which God so often gives, and which works so wonderfully for our relief, a good night's sleep. It is marvellous how the still, dark hours of the night will clear one's thoughts and bring him to his place; how often the dejection of evening is banished when the sun rises; how many mysteries and uncertainties have flown when the day comes back again. Elijah lay down to sleep and found that truth which is written in the Psalm, that God giveth to his beloved while they sleep. He gave to this man, for Elijah was his beloved. As he slept the angel touched him and spoke to him, and when he was awake he fed him. Twice he touched him, twice he roused him, and gave him bread and drink, and the man went forty days and nights on the strength of this ministry of mercy and of bread. We find no more the wish that he might die, no more the desire to be rid of the world, no more of the terrible despondency which made his earthly future full of terror. He went his way to the place where a greater than he had been commissioned, where Moses had found God, where God had found Moses. In the shadows and among the very cliffs of Horeb did this man wait until he should hear God; and he heard God. Men always hear God when they listen. He heard God, not in the wind which broke the rocks in pieces, not in the earthquake which shook the mountains to their base, not in the fire which blazed from cliff to cliff and lighted up the deep gorges; not in these. There had been enough of tumult, enough of storm and tempest. They had exhausted their power on this man's heart. God came closer to him, and when he had made quietness he spoke to him in a still small voice which Elijah heard. Now what is Elijah's complaint? "I only am left, and they seek my life to take it away." What is the remedy? God did that which another had purposed to do; he took the man's life away; not the breath out of his body, but his life. He took Elijah's life up into his own hands, and Elijah consented to have it taken up into the hands of God. I pray that it may be marked, because it is a lesson in which we need very much to be instructed, that God came to this despondent man, not with words of mere comfort, not with that worn and unsatisfying solace which we so often speak, not weeping with him, not weeping over him; but with that comfort wherewith men are comforted of God. He came to him with something to do. What did he say to this man who felt that his life was in peril, that he only was left and that men were about to take away his life? He did not point him to the glory which shall be forever; he did not say, "Well, Elijah, everybody must die, and it matters very little whether it is to-day or to-morrow, whether it is in this way or in that." He did not say, " You have rendered a very good service; you have outlived your usefulness." He said nothing like that. O, men, there is something here, in the way in which God came to Elijah, that is full of comfort and wisdom for you and me. For I notice this: That when God comforts a man, it is very often by giving him work. He does not content himself with soothing and quieting men as if they had no strength and were simply like crying children needing to be fondled and indulged. God respects the manhood of a man. What does he say to Elijah's complaint— "I, even I only am left, and they seek my life to take it away?" "Go, return on thy way to the wilderness of Damascus; and when thou comest, anoint Hazael to be king over Syria; and Jehu the son of Nimshi shalt thou anoint to be king over Israel; and Elisha the son of Shaphat of Abel-meholah shalt thou anoint to be prophet in thy room." That was God's comfort, something to do. When a man is busy for God he has comfort. Our despondent hours are the hours when we are not at work, or not at work for God. With a man's hands pouring oil upon Hazael and Jehu, and dropping the mantle upon Elisha, there is very little time to think about Jezebel. The calmness of God comes to the obedient child of God.

Then God took his life. It is very singular that this man, who had such a great fear that his life was to be taken away, that he was to die a death of violence, did not die a death of violence; did not die any death, not even on his bed. There came a chariot of fire and horses of fire when they were ready, and the prophet went up into the glory of God. The Lord had sought his life and had taken it away. How grand the contrast is! Let nine hundred years pass by. He was in the wilderness, this prophet strong and severe, clothed in his garment of camel's hair, feeding upon locusts and wild honey, the prophet of a rugged time committing his way unto God. Next you see him at Hermon, far in the north. This lonely man, who has found Moses somewhere beyond the clouds, comes down with Moses to the transfiguration of the Lord, no longer stern in spirit, or clad in coarse apparel. These two prophets of the ancient time appeared in glory and talked with the Lord " of his decease which he should accomplish at Jerusalem." Let us mark that the turning point of Elijah's life was not when he conquered the four hundred and fifty prophets of Baal, nor when he ascended in a chariot of fire into heaven; the turning point of this man's life was when, among the peaks of Horeb, he heard the voice of God and obeyed it, and putting his fears into the cave, went down to anoint Hazael to be king over Syria, and Elisha to be prophet in his room. It is not strange that ever afterwards the people were expecting Elijah to come back. You find it running all through their history. When Jesus came, it was Elijah, some said. Some declared that John the Baptist was indeed Elijah. The prophet so stamped himself upon the minds and hearts of the people that they looked for his return. If he ever had come — and he did in his time — it would have been because in the rock he heard the voice of God and did what God told him to do.

I have brought this to your notice this morning, not that I may speak upon this illustrious man, but because there are certain points here which, so far from being exceptional, are a common heritage for us. I wish to take one or two things out of this man's life, that we may see how our lives are to gather the inspiration for which this word is written.

These two things are to be noticed, and they are the points about which all I shall say will arrange itself; first, that this man had a life, just one life, and he had it all to himself there in the mountain. There were seven thousand other men who had seven thousand other lives, but he had this life and it was all his own; it was all the life he had. It was worth a great deal to him. He justly thought that it was worth a great deal to the world, to God; and he wanted to keep that life and make the most of it. Then the other thought immediately connected with this is, that he kept this life and made the most of it by finding God and linking his life with God's life; his plan with God's plan. If there are any two truths in the whole circle of truth which may be called universal, I think they are these: that every man has one life, and that every man shall make the most of that life by joining it with God's life and God's thought.

This is true of every one of us, that every man has his life, one life, and that life is fast slipping away from his grasp. How rapidly it is passing, year after year, and day after day! How little time it takes to make the hair white and the step feeble! How soon it comes, and our friends begin to say that we are getting old, and a little after we feel it ourselves, and by and by we give up one thing and another, and see that life is passing gradually away, until at last they carry us out and round the sods over us. Another thing is true. We have but this one life and this life is fast escaping; but we are to remember that this life is the making of the endless years beyond. I have said here a great many times, that there is but one life, and that time and eternity are one. But I wish this morning to take up our common method of speech. Let us speak as if life came to a great change in that which we call death.

This life, or the part of our life this side of death, reaches forward into that which is to come. We might expect this. It is after the analogy of nature. Life everywhere is after this plan. In the field there is the seed time, and after that the harvest. Following that analogy which the Scripture takes up and illustrates and enforces, this life is the seed time and after it comes the harvest; so that clearly this life finds its great value as it reaches on into the years which are before us. The Scripture teaches us in many places, that for the deeds we are doing here in the body we shall give account when we stand at the judgment seat of Christ. There is one other thing at this point: that life is not merely a system of existence, a series of days and nights flowing the one into the other, but that it comes to us with a certain meaning, a character of its own. One word must be taken as the expression of this meaning. The true character of life is well summed up in the word duty; it is that which we express by our word ought — what men ought to do. Duty is the meaning of life. The reason you live is that you have duty. Do your duty and you are following the law of your life; neglect your duty and you are wasting your life. So that a man finds this which joins him to himself, and to his fellow-men, so far as his duty touches them, and by this word duty, or ought, joins himself to God from whom the duty has come.

I am bringing you not a lesson of death, but a lesson of life. I want to have the great lesson not something which shall make us afraid of the end, but that which shall make us calm in view of the end, as we look upon any great work which is required of us and are not afraid of it because we know that we are equal to it. We should take up life in this hearty way, and think of it as something which we are wise enough to receive and manly enough to use even to its great fulfilmemt.

This word of the prophet at Horeb describes in its two parts the position of every one of us. We may see where he is, and what he feels. He is alone in the mountain, he and his life together, and he feels this: "I am the only one to take care of my life. I have no brother to care for it. I have no servant here to defend it. There is no prophet, there is nobody in all Israel, who feels as I do, or cares whether I live or not. I stand alone, keeping my life. That is, in some measure, the position of every one of us. We are alone. We have our kindred, we have our neighbors and our friends; but every one stands by himself, he and his life together. Every one besides, of the hundreds now in this house, might die before noon, and you live, my friend. They all might be happy and you sad; they all might be sad and you happy; they all might be right and you wrong; they all might be wrong and you right; God might approve every one of them and not you. God might be pleased with you and with no one besides. Thus separate does a man stand, with his own body, with his own breath, with his own duty, with his own need, with his own record on high and the destiny which follows the opening of the book. This is a commonplace truth, yet it may serve us well. Once for all we have a chance to live. The eternal years are committed to us, with one opportunity, extended by God's grace, to see if we will do God's will; and if that gracious opportunity is lost, there is no return. The cold waves rush in upon the gray rocks, and break against them, whoever lives, whoever dies,—

> But the tender grace of a day that is dead
> Will never come back to me.

Then there is the other point. "They seek my life to take it away." One woman mad and revengeful, sought the prophet's life. How easy it was to flee from her to Horeb! But a thousand seek our life; there is no Horeb where we may shield ourselves. There is no wilderness into which we may plunge and escape from—not Jezebel from whom we could hide, but that which we call death. It follows us everywhere; there is no escape for us; the law of nature is pronounced; the forces of the world are working against us; our powers are becoming enfeebled; steadily we are growing old; with steady step we are approaching that last hour. The powers of nature and the ordinance of God are seeking our life to take it away. Brethren, there is no help for us. The archers are ready, the bows are drawn, the shaft is pointed; it is certain that they who are seeking our life will presently take it away. I ask that these things may be accepted not as terrors, but as simple verities upon which we are to fashion our lives. What shall we do, then?

Some have said "If this be so, let us eat and drink, for to-morrow we die." Others throw themselves upon despair and say, "What is the use of living?" One often brings up that satire in theory, though seldom in practice, "What is the use of my saving money? I cannot carry it with me into another world. I must die penniless, like the beggar. What is the use of my trying to get any position? I have no sooner gained it than I am dead. What is the use of my trying to enjoy life? What matters it? Presently it will all be over, and I shall go away with my empty hands. More than I have gained I must leave. You tell me that I ought to be industrious and prudent and saving:

will you tell me what is the use of my heaping up treasure knowing not who shall gather it, or trying to be anything, or do anything in the world which to-morrow may forget that I ever lived?

> The saddest grave
> That ever tears kept green must sink at last
> Unto the common level of the world;
> Then o'er it runs a road.

What is the use?" I think there is much to be said on the side of the old preacher who had been a common man and a king, and had touched life on every side, and who wrote, "Vanity of vanities, all is vanity."

But the Scripture comes to us with quite a different lesson from that, and it speaks to us after this wise: "You are to-morrow to die; be very careful, therefore, what you eat and drink. You are to-morrow to go out of the world: be very careful, therefore, what you do while you are in the world. To-morrow you are to give account of that which you are doing here: therefore be very careful, and as this is the only life, the only opportunity, guard its moments well. Treasure them; let not life run to waste; let not any part of life run to waste. It is all the life you have; it is hurrying away; guard it; watch it day and night; watch it at every point, for it is your only life, and they are seeking to take it away." It is in view of these truths that the grandeur of life comes in. You will notice this; that a great man's life is great in some emergency, at some special point, or in the presence of a great work. A man who simply goes on his way and does easy things passably well, and is reasonably content, is not one who really masters the world. There comes to every one of us in our different places, and in different degrees according to our strength, some times when we must concentrate all we have upon one issue. And it is in this solitary opportunity that the force of our life comes out, and we put our manhood to the proof, and settle it with ourselves whether we are able and willing to live.

It is in this way that it comes to us now; if you feel that you have here many years, and that at any time you can recover the past, and gather up your life and make up for lost time, you will never do very much. The meaning of all this is, that you are standing at a critical point. This may be the turning point of the battle. Lose Waterloo, and it is St. Helena. Fail in this enterprise, and it is bankruptcy. Be broken down in this work, and it is defeat. Let this one life fail, and it is all over, it is all gone. There is no second chance. Life will never come back. You stand alone with your life. That supreme moment comes when you must determine whether you can face the one occasion, and in one life win eternity. It calls for all your reason, and all your conscience, and all your strength. If a man is a man, he gains the day as Elijah did. If he is careless and weak, he drifts though life until he drifts to the judgment of the ages that are to come.

We are inconsistent. Our views of life do not accord with our practices in life. Thus we say very truly that the most valuable thing we have is our life. "Millions of money for an inch of time,"— it was not one woman only who said that; ten thousand men and women have said it. Part with everything rather than die — of course everything but honor. It was a remark of one who knew men well, because he had searched them out in malice and cunning, who had gone up and down the earth with his shrewd, envious eyes, when he brought his testimony and laid it before God — "All that a man hath will he give for his life." And our Lord Jesus Christ, when he wished to express the greatest thing which a man would do, said: "Greater love hath no man than this: that a man lay down his life." That is the value of life; and when Jesus wanted to speak of that great gift of his own, he could find no better word than that, and said: "I give unto them eternal life." We value life because we enjoy it, and are in the habit of esteeming it highly, and hope for future good, and because there is a dread of the unknown. It is a part of our character that there should be this shrinking from the thought of change. A good old man once said to me, "I am not afraid of being dead, but I am afraid of dying." So it comes about in many ways that we think, and think truly, that nothing which we have is so valuable as life. Now see the inconsistency. What do we do with life? This best thing very many utterly waste. They never think upon its value, or upon its meaning, or upon what they are to do with it. They simply let the whole of it run away: it goes to waste. Still more marked is the wasting of parts of it. To think of wasting one of these invaluable days, one hour of the few and fleeting hours of life, when we have not fortune enough in all our house to buy back a single moment! We let the moments go as if we had them in plenty, or could get all we want in the market-place. We part the most easily with that which we value most, and which never can be recovered.

It was a most expressive illustration of the matchless English preacher, that men suffer life to slip through their hands as water slips through a marble fountain. He drew a picture of the marble image you have so often seen at the fountain, standing "steadfast, serene, immovable," with the water flowing through its lips.

It flows and flows, and the marble never thinks that it is flowing, never seeks to check it, never seeks to govern it. It flows on, and the marble hands never can take it back. So, he says — and how truly, how forcibly — we stand and let our time slip away. An hour and an hour, a day and a day, a year, and ten years, and twenty years, and fifty years, and seventy years, slip through the marble image which is a marble image still. Is not that true? Where is your yesterday? Did you clutch every moment as it came? Did you hold it as it sought to get away from you, making sure you had the whole of it, and that it was serving you well? What has become of your years? Have they gone as the water through the marble lips? Let me change the illustration, and say that life should come to us and pass from us as life comes to the growing grain which, springing from the seed, reaches up and takes every moment, takes every breath of air, all the sunshine and rain, all the dewdrops, covetous, eager, watching all the day and sleeping never at night, putting out its hands everywhere, that it may draw in out of time all the merit of time that the husband-man may reap the golden grain which shall reward his pains. Life comes to us somewhat in that way, to be taken up into our thoughts, made a part of ourselves, and put to those high uses wherein it may serve us forever.

What shall I say, then? Allow me to say these things! What shall I do in life, seeing that I have but one life, and they are seeking that to take it away? I will do these three things:

First, I will find the meaning of life. Life is more than a stream of water, or a stream of moments. Conscience and life belong together. What is my life to-day in its relation to my conscience? I am here with all my powers. What does life mean as it touches my powers? I am here among my fellow-men. What does my life mean in its relations to my fellow-men? I am here before God and his judgment. What does life mean in its relation to God and the judgment? I must find what it is, what is in it, what is the intent of it, what is the use to be made of it. I must know the meaning of my years. I may have no opinion about currency, about law, about anything else; but the one thing which I must know is, what it means to me that I am living to-day, and that these hours are slipping through my hands.

Secondly, I must take life up and put it to those uses wherein it serves me best. There comes that serious moment which finds us all, yet is not improved by us all, when a man makes choice of that which he will do in life; when he chooses, as we say, his profession. Some men choose their profession; I believe in many cases the professions choose the men. There are some men who are larger than life and greater than the world, who say, "I will not ask the world what it will let me do; I will ask myself, I will ask God, what I am made for, and I will choose my work according to my will and the will of God." It is a serious moment when a man makes up his mind whether his seventy years shall be spent here or abroad, whether in getting or giving; whether in getting a living or in making other people live; whether they shall be used in the service of self, or shall be spent in the service of God. It becomes a weighty matter, and the wise man must determine for himself what he shall do with the grand current of his life and with special parts of it. What shall I do today? These hours are winged, and are moving forward. These moments of your time which I am now occupying never will return. I feel the responsibility; perhaps you do. We must make something out of this hour. Do not be marble statues and let this Sunday forenoon run through your hands. Lay hold of it. Take it and use it. And, then, look on with life. We do not make the most of our college life, for instance, if we think that the day of graduation is all there is. We are studying for the future, reaching on, perhaps with definite plans, perhaps with general plans; but still with the future in our mind. All our life is to go forward beyond this graduation into the endless years. So Christ teaches us. Lay up your treasure in heaven, he says. "To him that overcometh will I grant to sit with me in my throne." "In my Father's house are many mansions. I will come again and receive you unto myself."

There comes finally this other thought, that what we are to do really in this one life of ours is to find God, or let God find us. I wish to say a word to the little children who are here. It is too simple for anybody else to listen to. Will the others think of what I have said while I say this word to the children? That man who knows best what a watch is good for is the man who made it, and the one who knows best what a life is good for is the One who made it. God made your life. God gives you your time, your thought. What you ought to do God knows best. Do you want to know what to think, what to choose, and how to make the most out of your years? Do you want to know what you are made for? Well, ask the Maker. Ask God. He will tell you what he wants you to be, what he meant when he gave you this life, and what he will have you do with it. Oh, God is so good! He likes to take us by the hand, and say, "My dear boy; I want you to do this." When God teaches us, then we get very wise, and when God helps us we are strong, and when God keeps us we are safe.

I ask, then, all who are not too old to be children, to come to God and find the meaning of life, and the strength to live it. You will hear a voice calling you; it will not be in the wind which moves along the streets, and bears the wisdom of this world; it will not be in the earthquake, which seems to shake society; it will not be in the fires which men are kindling on the hill-tops. The voice of God comes to us, still, small, reaching our heart, and then whispering steadily, always the same word, "Thou shalt love the Lord thy God; thou shalt do the things which are pleasing in his sight." Over against this oneness of our life stands the oneness of our God; and over against this singular, solitary responsibility stands the singular grace of God. Our thoughts are not to be divided, our trust is not to be parted. There is only one name under heaven given among men whereby we can be saved. There is only one law for our life, only one duty; there is only one Saviour. We need not waste a moment choosing between God and Mammon, between Christ and the world, between Christ and ourselves. Life is too hurried, life is too precious for us to have two Redeemers between whom our wandering thoughts must roam. We have one God, one life, one Saviour, one Judge, one eternity. Among these special and singular days do we make up our thoughts and plans;

and when we commit our life to God, he takes our purposes into his purposes; he takes our life into his keeping and guides us by his counsel.

I hear this morning the moving of the chariot wheels of God, the chariot of fire and the horses of fire. They are coming this way. They stopped in the last week at one of our homes, and a saintly spirit went up into the rest of God. The chariot of fire and the horses of fire, they will stop at the door of the men who love God and have used this one life worthily, and he who is ready shall ascend into the chariot and rise into the city of God which is forever, unto the everlasting youth, into the eternal years; for God has taken his life that he may give it to him in the glories of immortality.

II.

WHO LOVED ME.

SCRIPTURE LESSON: *Romans* viii: 14-39.

TEXT: Who loved me, and gave himself for me. *Galatians*, ii: 20.

THERE was an apostle who delighted to speak of himself as "that disciple whom Jesus loved." It was not that man who wrote the words which have now been read to you. Yet quite as much as his brother did St. Paul exult in the love which Christ had for him. Indeed, these words are a better expression of love than those which are used by the beloved disciple. St. John seems almost to shut out others; "that disciple," he says, as if there were no others whom Jesus loved. This apostle is broader in his thought. He draws in the love of God to himself; he feels how much more it is to him than it is to the world; he takes it to himself as if he stood alone; yet he does not shut out the world from the affection which Christ offers to all for whom he gives himself. The words of St. Paul are broader, again, in that they contain the method in which this love of Christ manifests itself. When St. John called himself "that disciple whom Jesus loved," or at the period in which he places those words, the great manifestation of the love of Christ had not been made. When St. Paul wrote, Christ had given himself to the cross, and the love had manifested itself in its own way. Therefore he wrote more fully as he rejoiced to write, "Who loved me and gave himself for me." Indeed, the expressions which St. Paul uses touching the love of Christ are all of the strongest character. He finds words insufficient as he rises into the vast regions which are beyond language, and beyond thought even. Thus, in his mind, the love of Christ while it is something to be known, "passeth knowledge," and reaches infinitely far away. Again, this love of Christ which comes to him is not something which touches his life, and with which he has no communion; but it is something to which his own heart is so bound that it is not possible for anything in this world, or in any world, to part the two asunder. Again, this love which Christ gives to him is a love which not only brings him the victory, but, going beyond that, bestows more than the victory, for, "we are more than conquerors through him that loved us." And again, this love which Christ has for him is not only a love which incites him to good deeds, and inclines him to do those things which please

Christ, but it comes with its constraining and compelling force, until he feels himself taken in hand by a strong power, and carried on to that which Christ requires of him. We have but to read these thoughts wherewith St. Paul expands the love of Christ, this sentence in which he declares that Christ loved him, to find how marvellous is this conception, how profoundly it is settled in his soul, and how wonderfully it is governing his life.

If we ask when it was that this love was given to him, the thought rises yet more in our minds as we remember that this love of Christ was before Christ died for him, and when this apostle was not his friend. The man was indifferent to him; the indifference grew into hostility; the hostility broke into violence of the most cruel and relentless kind. Yet Christ gave himself for one who did not love him, and continued to give himself, and give his affection, when St. Paul had become the violent persecutor. We find this affection coming to him, and working out for him this help through the cross, at a time when, if we are to trust our own thoughts, he might be reached in some other way. For St. Paul was an honest and amiable man, an upright man, and a religious man after the custom of his fathers, and very devout and very scrupulous in his religion; and it was when he was religious, and when he was honest, that Christ loved him and gave himself for him. His life had turned aside; he was misunderstanding Christ. What was needed more than that the Spirit should come to him and inform him in a quiet way who Christ was, and, working within the recesses of his soul, turn his thoughts towards Christ, and his life into the service of Christ? We are somewhat startled when we find that the want of this religious man is not met but by the Christ; that the want of this upright man is not met by any instruction or any spiritual power, but only by the compassion of Christ who loved him. "I, who am careful in my religion beyond all men — a Hebrew of the Hebrews — I claim this mercy of the Christ, who, that he might save me, loved me and gave himself for me."

I think we can make a creed out of these words, and a very large creed, and a very deep and rich creed, whose articles might run somewhat in this way: I believe in the Lord Jesus Christ who is strong enough to give himself for me. I believe in my necessity that the Son of God should give himself for me. I believe in the love of Christ which impelled him to give himself for me. I believe in a godly life which can be lived by the faith of the Son of God "who loved me and gave himself for me." I believe in a destiny of everlasting wealth and eternal blessedness which will be given to me for the sake of him "who loved me and gave himself for me." How large a confession it is; how profound an utterance of his acknowledgment! What an expression of his reverence, of his faith, of his contrition, of his hope, of his rejoicing! The whole expansion of his thought, the whole love of Christ, is condensed into this single sentence which spreads before us like the light of heaven, " Who loved me, and gave himself for me."

It was very natural that the working out of this principle in the mind of the apostle should be what it was. Even without reading his history we know what must come of this which he has here told us. These three things must come, certainly.

It must come to pass, first, that he will love the one who has loved him and given himself for him. There is but one thing which the loving heart is content with giving, and that is love. There is but one thing which the loving heart is content to receive, and that is love. It is an absurdity to offer anything less: it is an injustice to receive anything less. Even in our common relationships here there is but one thing which matches love, and that is love. A marriage between love on the one hand and money on the other is an abomination in the sight of God and man. Friendship which is between affection on the one hand and service on the other is a mockery and a shame. Piety which is between God's love on the one hand and a man's regard for the commandments on the other is not rational; is not acceptable to the man's conscience, and is not received in the court of Heaven. But one thing fits to love; but one thing contents love, either in the receiving or in the giving, and that is love itself. It is not until one comes to give this answer that he is very deeply conscious of that to which he is making his response. I suppose the reason that St. John applies to himself the words which, so far as we have any record, no one else applied to him, "that disciple whom Jesus loved," was that he had a constant conviction that he was that disciple who loved Jesus. How much Peter loved he did not know; how much Andrew and Thomas loved he could not tell; but he knew by every beating of his heart, by all the force of his thought and his love, that he loved Christ, and by that token he knew that he was the disciple whom Jesus loved. For it is inevitable when this man comes into the consciousness that Christ loves him, that his love should flow out as nothing else could draw it; that he should know there is nothing less that he can give; there is nothing less that Christ will receive.

Then there will come from this, in the second place, a trusting. It is impossible that one should know Christ and love him without trusting him, because he seeks to be depended upon according to that which he comes to do, and that which he promises to do, and that which we need to have him do. We cannot feel that he will fail us. The teaching of the apostle comes with force, and always awakens one response: "God who gave his Son for us will give us everything that we need. Christ who gives himself for us will not withhold anything we need. It is enough that he beholds the necessity. Even there our Lord himself left it: "Your Father knoweth;" that is enough. Your Father loveth; that is enough. Therefore the man trusts him for the present and for the future. It is out of this consciousness of a common love that he comes into that sublime confidence: "I know whom I have believed." Well, what is he, who is he? Who is this whom you believe? "I believe in him who loved me and gave himself for me; and I know that I shall receive a crown of righteousness in that day, for he who will give me the crown has already given me himself." He knows there can be no wasting of this love. Feeling within that his love for Christ can never change, he is yet more persuaded that the love of Christ can never change. Indeed, he might write out his own thought in the words of that English woman who has sung so well of the permanence of the love of Christ, the continuance of his affection for us:

"Oh, never is Loved ONCE,
  Thy word, thou Victim-Christ, misprized friend;
Thy cross and curse may rend;
  But having loved, Thou lovest to the end!"

And he would make answer, still in the words of this sweet singer:

"Those never loved,
Who dream that they loved once."

I think that by all which is true in the sacred affections of our hearts, we believe that if there is anything about us which will last, it is our love for that which is lovely. The old doctrine, so pleasant even in the sound of its words, of the perseverance of the saints is nothing but the doctrine of the permanence of love. As long as Christ's love is true and fresh, they who love him once love him forever. You ask the assurance that we shall enjoy his presence forever: it is that we love him here to-day. I know that it seems sometimes as if love had passed away. It may be because it never existed; it was a mere emotion not worthy of that God-word, love. It may be that it is merely obscured, as sometimes that which is recent comes in to cover that which is dearer to our hearts. Still, the singer is true, and the Christ is true, and your hearts are true: "Those never loved who dream that they loved once." They who feel within them the assurance of an unchanging love for Christ need no argument to prove to them the unchanging love of Christ for them; and upon that they rest their hope in quiet trust.

Then there follows a third thing, of course, and that is, the pleasing Christ. For the love at once seeks to do that which will gratify the one who is loved, recognizing this out of its own experience, that there is nothing so exacting as love; that we always demand the most of those we love the best; that we are always the most solicitous for the welfare of those who are dearest to us. You are more anxious that your child should do his best than that my child should do his best. You always hold up the highest standard before him who is nearest to you, and expect from him the most truthfulness, the most kindness, and the most devotion. Yet on the other hand there is nothing so small, if it be heartily given, that it is not dear to you — the flower which your child has picked from the wayside, the bright stone which he brings in out of the road, the simple utterance of his affection, the simple clasping of his arms about your neck. There is nothing too small for love to take, there is nothing too great for love to ask. One who knows this, finding it in the love of Christ for him and his love for Christ, at once feels that nothing can be too great that he shall do; that he can count all things but loss for the excellency of the knowledge of Christ Jesus his Lord, and count all things easy which shall please him who pleased not himself.

The apostle has come here upon the law of life. The one principle of life is stated in the strong and precious words before us. First, this is in God's life, for God is love. God is more than love; God is light also. God's love is not centred and restrained within his own heart; it must go out, or it is not love; it must give itself, or it is not love. He is not content with living and moving eternally in the sphere of his own affection, but his love must reach out to men, to every one who lives. Hence, if God loves men he must go out to men; he must meet them where they are; he must meet them in their necessities and do for them what love requires. If at any time it becomes necessary, he must put himself in sacrifice for men. I wish that we might see the marvellous reaching out of this simple truth. It was the fine saying of a man whom we all delight to honor, who never stood with more majesty than when recently among missionaries and the friends of missions he declared the sufficiency of the love of God, and uttered that sentence which might well be committed to our memory as a fact of history and a prophecy for all that is to be. "Christianity proclaims," he said, "in three words, of one syllable each, the grandest discovery ever made, the sublimest truth ever uttered." There are but three words in the language which answer that description. There are but three words in the Bible which can come to your minds in that connection — the grand, divine, eternal truth that "God is love." It is God's love that is his life. Take it away, and you have taken away so much from God; you have taken God from God. The principle of God's life within himself, the principle of God's life among the angels and among men, is the principle of a love which goes out and finds men, and blesses them according to their need. Hence, if one asks in Gethsemane why it is not possible that the sacrifice may pass away, there is but one answer. If it is a matter of will, it can pass away. Why cannot the cup pass unless it be drained by the Christ? Simply because those whom God loves need to have it drained. Love will stop at nothing. If men can be blessed by seeing the grapes upon the vine, let it be so; if they can be blessed with maxims of ethics and philosophy, let it be so. The time has come when those whom God loves can only be blessed *in that cup;* therefore it is not possible that the cup should pass away until it has been drained. And the reason it is not possible is, that God is love.

We come again upon this principle of life in our Lord Jesus Christ, who is here in the world as the embodiment of the thought: "God so loved the world that he gave his only-begotten Son." Christ so loved the world that he came into it, and went about with ministries of mercy, until at last he stretched out his hands upon the cross, loving men and giving himself for men. Take away the love from Christ and what have you left? Possibly the teaching, perhaps the purity of his life; perhaps an example white as marble, and moral maxims cold as snowflakes and as little nourishing to the heart. The one thing which makes Christ dear to you, the Saviour, the Comforter, the Helper, is that the life of Christ is love.

Hence, obviously, when you come to the Christian life the principle is the same. There is but one life in Heaven and in earth, and that is God's life. The life that we live in the flesh is the life of God in us; and when we come to the Christian life, it is the life of Christ. There never was but one Christian life, and that is Christ's life. I will not play with words. If one chooses to say that this is a Christian nation, and that men can be Christians though they do not believe in Christ, very well. They are not the Christians of the New Testament. You know the testimony of the poor Chinaman at the West who found himself abused, insulted in the streets, beaten and stoned, and who wrote back the piteous tale in his simplicity: "The men who did it are Christians, but they are not Jesus-Christians." Now the only "Jesus-Christians" in the world are the Christians in whom Jesus is. It is only as Christ is in us that we are Christians; it is only as Christ's life is in us that we have the Christian life. Even as it flowed out from the hands and the lips and the spirit of Jesus of Nazareth must it flow out in our lives, in all that we do and in all that we are, as we go our way through the world. It comes to take us up and control us and exalt us forever — the one Christian life. I can come to Christ as the greatest of teachers and sit calmly down to receive his instructions; I can come to him and mark the purity and simplicity of his example; I can follow him until I am attracted by the charity and benevolence of his spirit; but I have not found the Christ. No man whose heart was ever full of the love of Christ was content to say, "Who loved me and taught me the Sermon on the Mount;" "Who loved me and healed the sick and raised the dead;" "Who loved men and taught them by a holy example that he could do what they could never do." No Christian heart talks in this way. It is the heart far away from him which says it; it is the Christian, perhaps, but it is not the "Jesus-Christian." "Thou shalt call his name Jesus, for he shall teach men to pay their debts," — who said it? Never the Christ, never the disciple, never the man whom Jesus loved. "Thou shalt call his name Jesus, for he shall save his people from their sins." Now we know what St. Paul means: "Who loved me and gave" — not his words, not his miracles, — "who gave himself for me." I gather up his teachings and all which is matchless and precious in his life, in this one gift; for when I have my friend, I have my friend's house, I have his words, I have his example, I have his love; I get all when I get him; I get everything which any one else gets, and I get more when I get the Christ who gave himself. Taking himself in his hands, he gave himself over to me and became mine, my own, my own Saviour. I do not believe that I shall ever learn, even from the Sermon on the Mount, the spirit which will make me kneel down before my Judas and wash his feet. If ever in God's grace I become able to do that, it will be because there stands before me the Christ girded with a towel, and with a basin of water in his hands, and love in his heart. I do not believe that I can ever go in self-forgetful devotion through the world because I know that Christ fed the multitudes and taught sweet lessons of charity. I do not believe that I can ever lose my life for Christ's sake while I content myself with gathering up his parables and taking their blessed lessons to my heart. But at the cross there is this spirit; in the cross I seek it; from the cross I take it. "I can do all things," do you say, "for I know that Christ stilled the tempest on the sea of Galilee, and I know that he said we should render unto Cæsar the things that are Cæsar's, and unto God the things that are God's?" Oh! do it if you can. If I am ever able, I believe if you are ever able, to make up a Christian life in the world, it will be under the constraint of that word which this man wrote : "I can do all things through Christ," "who loved me and gave himself for me."

I think we have found many instances besides those which are recorded in Holy Scripture where this principle rules. We need not go out of our own homes to find the controlling power of love, if not the freshness and the strength of it; the love which makes a man toil unto old age for those whom he loves; which makes a mother watch through the weary nights, nor mark the hours, for those she loves; the pure sparks from the glowing heart of God's affection. If we look at those who have stood out with marked lives of usefulness and devotion, we find this principle. That missionary mother separating from her children on a foreign shore, sending them away from her home that they might receive the nurture of her native land, and as the boat pushes out which is never to come back, lifting up her heart to say, "I do this for thee, Jesus," has a love like the love of Christ; "I do this for thee, Jesus, for thou hast left thy Father's house for me," that is her thought. Then there are those words of that noble man who wrote to his children in England, out of the heart of Africa, "Tell them I have left them for the love of Jesus, and they must love him too." Hear his cry, "O divine Love, I have not loved Thee strongly, deeply, warmly enough." "O Jesus, fill me with Thy love now, and, I beseech Thee, accept me, and use me a little for Thy glory." There is but one force which can do this; there is but one power which bears men into this divine usefulness; and the power lies within this brief sentence: "I do this for him who loved me and gave himself for me."

Friends, the lesson for every one of us is this — not for those without the Church more than for those within the Church; it is the great lesson for all men: — that if we are to live the life which is worthy of us, it must be as we receive the life of the Christ, and the Christ at his best. When your life moving up blends with his life, when the love of Christ comes into your heart to take possession of it, there can be but one result. It will save you, for Christ gives himself to save sinners; it will bring you up into the Christly life, for Christ comes, the vine, to give his life unto the branches; it will govern your thoughts, your purposes, your steps; it will exalt your life and sanctify and glorify your spirit; it will bring you at last into that grand fulfilment which the beloved disciple saw and could not describe: "We shall be like him, for we shall see him as he is." Whosoever sees Christ as he is, sees Christ loving him and giving himself for him. Oh! see it, friends; look until you see it; look until the sun goes down; look until the morning comes; wait, gaze, look, look with longing eyes until you see it! When that thought becomes your thought, when it takes hold upon you as a part of your life, then will God be glorified in you, and you will live in the faith of the Son of God who loved you and gave himself for you.

Let me turn as I close to the teaching of Christ himself — uttered not in Syriac syllables, nor in English sentences, which we might not understand, and whose power and beauty we might not perceive — the words of Christ spoken in this body of Christ which is here set forth again before us. There is Christ. Do you want to come close to him? You will find him there. He said that we must eat his flesh to have life; we must drink his blood to have life; we have not seen him until we have seen him on the cross; we have not found his love until we have found his love crucifying itself; we have not entered into his grace until his pierced hands have held us against the bosom of his divine, redeeming love.

They say sometimes in Scotland, in their quaint phrase, that the Lord's table is "fenced." You do not see the fence here; there is none — not a wall, not a door open or shut. There is but one guard around that table: a circle of light streaming out from the bread and from the wine, a circle of light around it, made of these divine words: "Who loved me, and gave himself for me." You must not think to step over it, to pass under it, to remove it. You draw near, and stooping down, you lift it in your hands, you hold it to your heart, and thus you come to the Lord's table, which is the table of your Saviour, and he gives you to eat and drink with him. There is no fence about the Church. On its threshold lies a single line: "Who loved me, and gave himself for me." Take it up in your hands and hold it in your heart and the

Church is open. The door of Heaven is always open. Across the threshold of Heaven there lies one line of light. You take it into your life and pass on with it to the throne, carrying it in your rejoicing, "Who loved me, and gave himself for me."

>Oh, dearly, dearly has he loved,
>And we must love him too,
>And trust in his redeeming blood,
>And try his works to do.

III.

CHOOSE WHOM YE WILL SERVE.

SCRIPTURE LESSON: *S. Matt.* vii: 13-29.
TEXT: Choose you this day whom ye will serve." *Joshua* xxiv: 15.

I MUST ask you to read the last two chapters of this Book of Joshua, to recall to your minds the circumstances under which these words were spoken. Joshua was an old man; his life as a chieftain and a statesman was about to end. He was giving his last words to the people. He did not carry them through the details of the life which they were to live; he did not give them commandments arranged in systematic order; he brought them rather to one point where they were to stand, and, standing there, or moving from that point towards God, they were to make up their life. He did not mean that they were to choose between one God and another, although the form of his words might suggest that. He knew there was not a man among them who would choose the gods of the Amorites, or the gods on the other side of the river, instead of

Jehovah. What he did was to state in a strong way their duty and privilege; that they should choose as he had done; that they should choose the Lord to be their God. Moses had been placed in somewhat similar circumstances on the day of the worship of the golden calf, when, standing before the people, he cried with a voice of indignation and reverence, "Who is on the Lord's side? Let him come unto me." Later than this, in the days of Baal, Elijah cried with the same spirit: "How long halt ye between two opinions? If the Lord be God, follow him."

It is evident that this mode of presenting the claim which God makes upon us is somewhat different from that in which it is usually presented. This form of words has very much passed out of use, and the thought which lies within the words has been in a measure superseded. We are not saying to-day, "Choose you whom ye will serve;" we are saying, "choose you whom ye will trust." We have passed over from this idea of a life which is to be lived for God to a life in which God is to take us up and carry us on, promising us Heaven, alluring us with pleasures all the way, and indulging our wishes at every point, if so be, in our condescension, we will consent to be saved. I think that it is for lack of the strong element which the Scriptures always present, that it is man's duty to obey God, our piety has fallen so much upon inefficiency; that it lacks nerve; that even our belief of the truth grows feeble and our obedience of the truth feebler; that our devotion to God is an uncertain thing, and our service almost as variable as our states of mind. We need to have breathed into our thoughts a feeling of duty; a sense of something which we must do; of a life which we are to live. I gather it all up into this saying of the old Hebrew statesman in which we are called upon to choose whom we will serve; to choose God and to serve him continually.

While the thought of trusting Christ and the offers of his grace appear so much in the New Testament, this thought of serving God is the underlying principle throughout. Our Lord never, in all his offer of rest and peace and mercy, lost sight of this. What was his most common idea of that life into which he called men? It was life in a kingdom. "The kingdom of God," "The kingdom of heaven," were his common phrases. Men are to live under the eye of a king and to obey him to the end. So, when he presented the kingdom of heaven with all its delights under the image of a marriage feast, it was not a feast spread by the wayside where men were working; it was not a table laid in the thickets where they might be reclining; it was a feast within the gates of the king's house. If any man ate of the feast, he came up out of the highways, passed through the door, entered into the place where the table was spread, and there took his place. Christ knew nothing of any joy for a man outside of the king's house. So it was with the parable of the prodigal son, in which our Lord did not promise certain joys to be had by remaining in the "far country;" he did not teach that there were for this wretch a robe, and a ring, and a kiss, and a fatted calf, and all the blessings of life, while he was by his own act an exile and wanderer, or that there was one of them anywhere but where his father was. If he was to be blessed as he wished, he must go home, and within his father's house he would find what was there alone — his father's blessing and his grace. Indeed, the whole thought of the redemption of Christ rests upon this. The cross of Christ springs indeed out of God's love, but it holds fast to this idea of the obedience of the soul to God. Christ bids men leave their boats and follow him — leave their lives and follow him. The order of events is like this: First, God and his will; then men obeying God's will and living in happiness and holiness; then men breaking with God's will and passing into sinfulness; then God coming to ransom men out of this state of sin and misery, and to bring them back into the state in which they were before, establishing them again in integrity that they might have the blessing of God. If we view this life, as we sometimes do, as a road, men have stepped off the road and wandered away from it. When God comes to them he does not point to a new path, or make a new highway for them; he brings them back into the old road, that, walking thereon, they may go to the end to which they would have gone if they had never turned away. This truth of obedience is in entire harmony with the tender thoughts applied to God. If we speak of God as love, we have asserted the strongest of all reasons why we should serve him. If we call God our father, we have declared at once the very reason why we ought to obey him and seek his pleasure in all things. If we speak of the love we have for God, we have declared the very principle which will make us do his will. The soul of obedience is love, and the body of love is obedience.

Passing from these primary considerations, let us notice a few things. In the first place, this: that the law of God, which is given to us to be obeyed, is the expression of the nature of God. There is a great difference between the law of God and the law of men. The law of God is a necessary law; it is simply his own nature opening itself out. It may very well happen, that a king may come to the throne and find the constitution and legislation all prepared. He may not like the constitution, but he must administer it; he may not approve the laws, but he must administer the laws. He is held to this although his own life and his own spirit may be at variance with the laws all the way through. It is not at all so with

God. God is before all constitutions and all statutes and all principles of life; and these principles are but the expression of himself. God is love: God's love utters itself. God is holiness; this holiness makes itself known in holy desires and holy commandments for the children of men. It is very much like the sun and its light. The sun gives light because it is the sun; it is the nature of it to shine; and God gives commandments because it is his nature to give them. Do you not, even as earthly fathers and mothers, tell your children what you know they ought to do? That is a little of the same principle which makes God tell you and me what we ought to do, because this is the right thing to do; because this is the pleasant thing to do; because this is the profitable thing to do, but above all because this is the right thing to do. So long as God is God he must tell us what to do; so long as God is holy, he will tell us holy things to do; so long as he is God, we ought to do those things which he gives us to do. Indeed, it is simply out of the question that we should have God without having his commandments. To return to the figure of the sun, you do not get the benefit of the sun unless you get its light. Without that the orb yonder in the heavens is little to you. They have been reckoning up its distance, whether it be ninety-two or ninety-five millions of miles away. It might be a million times further than it is; it is nothing to you, unless it gives you something and you take that something. It is little to you that there is a God yonder, unless something comes down from him so that you can take hold of it; unless his law comes down, and you know what to do; unless his strength comes down, and you are able to do it. Without the gift, it is to small purpose that yonder shines the sun, or yonder reigns the God. God gives these laws which are a part of himself. He speaks, and it is commandment; he looks, and it is statute; he wishes, and it is law; he brings his great desires and counsels among men that we may take them and make our life out of them. It is simply God out of his own nature breathing his nature, as the perfume comes from the flower, as light comes from the sun, as fruit comes from the tree, as goodness comes from the good, breathing his own nature in commandments down among the children of men. "Choose you," says this old Hebrew statesman, "choose you to take the light of the sun; choose you to take the fruit of the tree; choose you to take the nature of God which along these lines of light comes down to you for your guidance and your comfort." It is not meant, again let me say, that we should choose between God and another. I suppose that to none of us does this choice present itself to-day in any tangible shape. However men may reason it out, whatever we may say in our homilies and exhortations, I presume it is not true of any one here to-day that he has chosen deliberately to serve any one except God. He may be serving some one else, but that ever he has said to any one else in heaven or earth, "Thou art my God and I will serve thee," is not to be believed. Yet it may come to pass practically that a man does serve another. We are not to consider here the relative value of this or that which he serves. My only interest to-day, brethren, is to beg you to choose God and to serve him. Whether it be Baal, or Ashtaroth, or the gods of the Amorites, is comparatively a small matter. Take any one according to your fancy, if from among these you are to make your choice. But with all earnestness I pray you to choose the only one whose right it is to reign; the only one whom you have a right to serve.

The choice of a principle and method of life may be made by a natural and simple process. I may consult simply my own pleasure. I may say, "I will do those things which I wish to do." I am very likely to do this carelessly, floating on from day to day, planning to-day what I want to do to-day, waking to-morrow morning and planning again what I want to do in that day. In all I stand up as the object of my own thought and care. I may do this wilfully, or I may do it without a conscious volition.

I may choose to do what other men wish to have me do; I may do this deliberately, or I may do it out of an easy good nature which tries from hour to hour to please my friends. I may choose to do what others are doing; I may do this deliberately, or I may do it by that force of imitation which makes me, in my amiability, follow in the steps of others. I may combine these. On some days I may serve myself and on some my fellows. I may vary these methods, or unite them into one, so that I can hardly tell whether I am living for myself or for humanity. There are many varieties of this idolatry. Against all of them stands out the one who alone is God, and the exhortation of the preacher is, " Choose the Lord God and serve him."

When a man has done this it is very evident that he stands in the way of righteousness and of blessing. I have said little thus far of that which we term Christianity; I have said nothing about coming to Christ to be saved. Yet I wish to recall this single point, and I pray that this may be noticed now, before we pass to anything else. Choose God, Jehovah, the maker of heaven and earth, your maker, your father; choose him and serve him. Determine with yourself this: " Whatever God asks, whatever is his commandment, I will obey. Heaven and earth may pass away, I will be true to this. Come sunshine or storm, come wealth or poverty, come life or death, I will be true to God." They said to Napoleon when he was before a certain castle, "Sire, if you attempt to take this castle it will cost you the lives of ten thousand men." "Then I will give the lives of ten thousand men." So choose God. Men will tell you that it will change your life : very well. They will tell you that it will make you pray : that it will bring you into the church : very well. If it cost you ten thousand lives, pay them for your own life ten thousand times over. It is this for which I plead. Choose God always to be served, wherever he leads, whatever he forbids, whatever he requires. The man who shall do this stands with his face towards God, and with his life towards God; he stands in the way in which he shall be blessed. Very certain is it that God will come to this man ; that God's grace will find him. He may never have heard of Christ, but he will find Christ, or Christ will find him. The love of God looking upon him where he stands, will come flowing out of the heavens until it gathers about his feet and takes him up and he is borne away on the grace of Christ. There can be nothing which will commend a man more to the grace of God than the single purpose to do the will of God. The man who stands facing God will be found of God. I believe the great reason why men do not find God is because they are not looking for him. They say, "I will find his mercy ; I will find blessing at his hands; and after a time I will determine to serve him ; as if they said, " I will take a voyage to Europe after I have wandered over the mountains of Switzerland." There is but one thing first in any right life; there is but one thing first in any Christian career; and that is to choose God and pledge the life to him. Then God comes to help and save the man. The good shepherd seeketh the sheep upon the mountains to bring him down to the fold. If the shepherd be going one way, and the sheep, even with the purpose to find the fold, be going another way, they may never meet. If the shepherd is seeking the sheep, and the sheep is seeking the fold, and seeking the fold is going directly towards the shepherd, they will meet; they are sure to meet. If Christ goes out from God to find a man, and the man is coming towards God, they will come together. Two trains going in opposite directions on the same track are certain to meet. Christ coming from God and man going towards God are sure to meet. Therefore I say, set your face towards God and you are facing the approaching Christ. Indeed, if we take Christ's work itself, we find that the object of his life in the world was to bring men into this obedience to God. We have not estimated his work at all correctly or thoroughly unless we see that the outcome of it all was to bring men to God. It is a thoroughly false idea that Christ came into the world simply to make men happy, or simply to put men in one place rather than another. Christ came into the world to bring men back where

they always ought to have been; and he will
never be content till he has done this; and he
will never have saved a man until he brings
him there. You may throw yourself into the
water and drown, trying to save a drowning man;
but all your pains go for nothing so long as
the man remains under the water. I say it rever-
ently, the Son of God may die for sinners, but
so long as men continue in their sin he has died
in vain. The redemption of Christ may be able
to save men from sin unto the uttermost, but
so long as men will continue to sin they are
not saved. It is only as we come where we are
right with God that we are saved; and when
we are there, nothing can harm us. Do you not
mark that the shepherd when he goes forth for
the sheep, and finds him upon the mountains, does
not there pity him, weep over him, tearing his own
hands upon the thorns to make a pretty little fold
for him, and shelter him and feed him with the
scant herbage which grows in that frigid clime,
trying to make the sheep happy there? I believe
that is the idea which a great many people have
of Christ's work: that he comes down into this
poor, broken world and tries to make us contented
here; tries to take off a little of the cold, the sin,
the unrighteousness and unbelief; whereas Christ
never stays upon the mountain longer than is
necessary; he will not leave the lamb upon the
mountain, but take him in his arms or on his

shoulder and carry him down into the fold, and never stop until he is there. He is no friend to the prodigal, who, finding him down in the "far country," says, "Oh! man, this is a hard life; this feeding swine is unprofitable; I will give you a more comfortable situation near by; I will give you better wages. You are clothed with rags: I will give you good clothing; you are hungry: I will feed you"— he is no friend who says that. The only one who can befriend the prodigal is he who says, "Oh! man, come home. No matter what you do here; no matter how you fare here; no matter whether you are in rags and hungry, or not; you are wretched; you are wrong here; the only kindness I can do you is to carry you home to your father's house." That is the work of the Lord Jesus Christ.

I think you know that I believe in the kindness and love of Christ for men; but to make men contented in disobedience is not his kindness. To make a man happy before he has chosen to serve God, it is not right; it is not kind. It would be almost working against God himself if Christ tried to make us contented before we have chosen God that we may serve him. If Christ makes our homes happy without God, that we may be contented in them; if he soothes our sin, and takes off the grosser form of it, so that our conscience may not trouble us; he is no longer kind, for he is keeping us away from

God; keeping us still guilty; leaving us still lost. He is not kind until, dying for us, he takes us to bring us back to God. The work of Christ is that you and I may choose God and serve him.

What shall we do, then, we who know Christ's name to-day? I have spoken of those who might come to God not knowing Christ. We know Christ: what are we to do? Manifestly, we are to use what we know. If you know where a man is, then act as if you knew where he is. There are times when you want to find some one and you do not know where he is. You look for him in one house and another, one town and another, one country and another; but if you know where the man is, you go directly there. If you do not know where God is, search the heavens and earth until you find him. Suppose you want to find what a man's will is: you conjecture, you inquire, you ask in vain in a hundred places; but if you can find the man, by asking him you find what his will is. That is the right thing to do. We want to come to God using what we know; not setting aside our knowledge of Christ and his truth; not setting aside the Gospel as if we were to come to God without the Gospel. We take what we know. And what do we know? Why, we know that God is a great deal nearer to us than the stars are; we know that God is here in Christ his Son seeking to reconcile us unto himself. We want to find God, we who know

Christ. Then what shall we do? Why, come where God is closest to us, and that is in Christ. Find God where he is. Suppose I want to find you at this moment, because I have a message which I must give to you at once. Should I not be foolish if I should go to your house and call for you there, when I know all the time that you are here? Should I not be more foolish, if, trying to find God, I pass away from God when he is here, in Christ his Son, and look far away for him, wandering over the long path and seeking him at the distant door of Heaven? We shall find God where he is nearest.

I want to know the will of God because I want to do it: where shall I find it? Christ declares the will of God and illustrates it in his life. I come to him and learn it from him. Or, I want to find the grace of God; I want to know whether I, who have wandered away, can come back; whether I, who have done wrong, can be forgiven. I ask the astronomers on their nightly watchtowers to tell me what the Pleiades say, or what is written on the bands of Orion. Why should I not reverence the astronomer? But what are the stars telling? What can any one say of the grace of God save God himself? God comes with his grace and Christ declares it, and I come to him because he knows, and I want to know, whether I can be forgiven, and how I can be forgiven. Knowing Christ I come to Christ, because in

Christ God is nearest, because in Christ God's will is most plainly declared, because in Christ alone God's grace is manifest, and finding him I find God. This, then, becomes for us who are intelligent men to-day, who know of Christ and have his gospel, the one thing to do : to choose to serve God, and to choose God who comes to us in Christ, whose will is declared by Christ, whose grace in Christ works out our redemption.

But let me ask you to notice again, that this redemption in itself is not the place where we are to stop. It is to bear us on to something else. It is not the final stage; it is not our rest; it carries us on to something beyond it. Christ came to bring men to God ; and not until he has brought them to God and given them to God — God's ransomed children, who are henceforth to live with him and obey him — has he done his work. I know that beautiful line of the hymn ; I would not take a note from its divine and blessed melody. It is true, but, like most single lines, it is but a fragment of the truth : —

> Simply to thy cross I cling.

Yes ; with the arms of a clinging faith. I shrink from going on, lest any one should think I do not make enough of that which is the heart and life of piety, the simple trust in Christ and him crucified. But what did Christ ever say, what did the apostles ever teach, which warrants you in saying,

"All I have to do is to cling to the cross?" What did Jesus say about the cross? He said, "Take it up and go about obeying the will of God." Cling to the cross, not as one who is weary and is there finding rest alone; not merely as one who is guilty and is there finding pardon alone. Cling to it, doing the will of God. Where would the world have been to-day if John, and Peter, and Paul had been content to cling to the cross and do nothing more? You have God to serve, and a man cannot do all the will of God sitting in a sanctuary, kneeling in a closet, clasping his arms around a sacred tree, or laying his cheek against the wood that is red with the blood of the Christ of God. By Christ alone are we saved, and Christ we are to follow. Cling to the cross, but not "simply." Cling to the cross, but go about clinging to it. Cling to the cross, but obey God while you cling, following his commandments with your deeds, glorifying him upon the earth, finishing the work which he has given you to do. Cling to the cross until the eternal glory comes; but while you cling, follow Christ whithersoever he leads you.

If we are not to rest upon redemption, but to go through it to that which is beyond, still less are we to rest upon virtue. Let us pause long enough to pay a tribute of sincerest respect to honesty, truth-telling, charity, virtue. But should a man rest in these? Is it enough for a man that he be honest with all the men who live on streets running east and west, though he be not honest with men living on streets running north and south? Is it honest for a man to do what he ought with his neighbor, and not to do what he ought with his God? Is it right for a man to love his mother and not his father? Is it right for a man to love his father here and not his Father there? What is honesty? It is a poor, bruised, disfigured image of honesty which men bow down before, when all their life through they are dishonest because they do not serve God with their heart and with their life. There is no reason why a man should do the will of men which does not hold him to the will of God. The reasons which bind a man to love his father, hold him to the love of God. Why, then, rest in this which is almost sure to slip into vanity and self praise, the feeling that we are honest, paying our debts, dealing justly, and that this is enough? Poor father, I pity you if you have a thankless child! Sometimes I want to pity God for thankless children; for honest men who never pray, virtuous men who never love him, truth-telling men who never choose to serve him.

How beautiful are those Psalms, and the other passages of the old and new Scriptures which describe the life of a good man! How wonderfully have they been abused; as if one should take the jewels from the king's crown and tread them in the dust. The fifteenth Psalm:

"Lord, who shall abide in thy tabernacle, who shall dwell in thy holy hill? He that walketh uprightly, and worketh righteousness." Strange as it seems, men have even used that Psalm as a reason for not being Christians. They repeat its words and keep away from Christ. And that other verse: "What doth the Lord require of thee, but to do justly, and to love mercy, and to walk humbly with thy God." Men have even taken that as a reason for not loving Christ. "Fear God, and keep his commandments; for this is the whole duty of man" — "therefore we need not be Christians," some have said. Oh, the wrong, the injustice, the cruelty of it! These passages of Scripture all describe truly the estate of men when God is pleased with them, but they describe an estate into which we are to enter. Christ's work in the world is to enable us to enter into it. He comes that the fifteenth Psalm may be true of us.

Change the prophet's question. What doth the Lord require of thee in order that thou shouldst see the mountains and valleys of Switzerland? To go out in the morning and walk through valleys and over mountains with open eyes; that is all. Do it to-morrow morning, and will you see the Alps? What doth the Lord require of a man who wants to see the mountains but to look? Why, there is a small matter of getting to Switzerland which ought not to be neglected. "Lord, who shall abide in thy tabernacle?" — there is a

little matter of getting into the tabernacle before
you abide there. We enter by Christ's work. "He
that hath clean hands," we say calmly; but let us
remember that Christ has come to make our hands
clean. "Blessed are the pure in heart." Christ
came to make us pure in heart. When Christ's
work is done in us, then the Psalm becomes the
glad reality of our life. Let us never mistake the
end for the means, or the means for the end. God
would bring us into this righteousness, but the
way to come into it is by the choice of God, and
Christ the Son of God, our Saviour.

As I have thought upon these things there has
come to me again and again that incident in
Elijah's life, when he stood by the river through
whose parted waters he had just walked, and was
to be taken away. There appeared a chariot of
fire and horses of fire, and the Lord took the
prophet in the chariot, and carried him up into
the glory. I read it now as a parable; the
chariot of fire and the horses of fire remind us
of our Lord Jesus Christ who has come where we
are. The chariot is not heaven, but the horses
can take us up into heaven. "The chariot of
fire and the horses of fire" are from God, and are to
take us to God. We come to Christ, we enter
into Christ, and Christ bears us up to our Father's
house. Read that sentence of our Lord's own
words: "No man cometh unto the Father but
by me;" and this other sentence, which is less

familiar, "No man can come to me except the Father which hath sent me draw him." We have God seeking us, bringing us to Christ the Saviour, and then Christ taking us up into the tabernacle and temple of our God.

What do I beg for to-day, then? That with one act we will choose God, bringing our will to bear upon this act, using our thought and our life until we choose God and find him and dwell in his grace.

Can we do this? Can we not agree so far as this: that we will take the Lord to be our God? Can we agree upon this to-day, brethren, and then pass on to the study of God's will and to the results of it? Here, this morning, I speak to you and I speak to my own heart. Can we covenant with God so far as this, that we will serve him with all our heart and with all our life? He who shall come so far as that shall find the mercy of God bearing him up into the glory.

Now, as we go away, shall we sing a loyal hymn, the hymn of a loyal people, the hymn of true hearts singing unto their Lord?

All hail the power of Jesus' name.

IV.

LOOKING TOWARD THE SEA.

SCRIPTURE LESSON: *Acts*, xxvii.
TEXT: Go up now, look toward the sea: *I Kings*, xviii: 43.

THE prophet was waiting for rain. The cloud which was to bring it in abundance would come by the way of the sea. He sent his servant seven times that he might know if the cloud was coming. "Elijah went up to the top of Carmel; and he cast himself down upon the earth, and put his face between his knees, and said to his servant, Go up now, look toward the sea."

It is with a similar intention that men have commonly looked toward the sea. They have sought something from it. They have looked for benefits which must pass over it to reach them. They have taken its treasures. They have made it a highway for the ships which have carried their merchandise from land to land, and exchanged the products of separated climes. They have journeyed over it that they might visit lands of historic interest, or study the living institutions of the world. The shores of our own land were sought in ships which pressed their way across the sea, bearing the men who looked beyond the wide waters for a haven for their liberty and purity. This church, this college, this nation, came by the way of the sea.

Our greatest enterprises make an alliance with the sea and the men who belong to it. Ships must carry our missionaries to the ends of the earth, that they may erect in every land the cross of the Redeemer and the throne of the King. Our Lord himself preached from a fisher's boat, and called from the sea the men who were to be his first disciples and apostles. Men have been using the sea for their own purposes, always seeking and getting. The sea, the seamen, and the ships are the common benefactors of civilization and religion. Even now, as the summer days draw on, we are looking toward the sea for renewed health and enlarged resources of mind and heart.

It is time that we possessed and exercised a more generous spirit: that we asked if we cannot give where we have received so much; if we cannot respond to these good offices with our own thoughtful and liberal benefactions. With this thought and purpose in our minds, let us go up now and look toward the sea.

Looking off from this height, what do we behold? The vast expanse of waters, uniting the lands which they seem to keep apart, and making the lands a safe and pleasant dwelling-place for men; the seat of great nations; the abode of an advancing civilization. But it concerns us much more to observe that there are three millions of men whose dwelling is upon the sea. They are separated from their families, and from the comfort and security of their homes, from the enjoyments of friendly society, and from the ministrations of the church.

On the other hand, they are thrown into the severest hardships. Their work is hard, their peril is constant. Whether upon ship or on shore, they are in danger. Their calling and their training make them an easy prey. The lifetime of the sailor is twenty-eight years, and his sea life eleven years. The monotonous story of shipwrecks is the saddest reading of the winter months. Along much of the seaboard the old prophecy scarcely fails of fulfilment, that the women of Colias shall roast their corn with oars.

This is for us. The sailor is the indispensable man. Should he retire from service the world would almost stand still. Look at the manifold influence of Greece upon the world. The book which is the heart of the world's life, under whose sway humanity is to attain to its renown, was written by divine appointment in the language of Greece. But Greece lies within the seas, its winding coast breaking into harbors for the ships of the great sea. Greece was fitly likened to a ship, and Corinth, "the city of the two seas," was the prow and stern of the ship. In allegory, Corinth was a woman upon a rock between two other figures, each of which held a rudder. The symbol is well chosen. In the history of the world the ship and the sailor hold a conspicuous place.

These sailors are men like ourselves. They are brave, bold, generous, impulsive, open-handed and open-hearted men. They are the children of Our Father. Our duty is their duty. Before them stretch the endless years. The gospel of to-day and the judgment of the great day are for them. For them Christ died and rose again. They have minds which can be instructed, and souls which can be saved, and lives which can be set in highest service.

To the fishermen of Galilee the Saviour extended his personal ministry. A part of his going about doing good was on the sea. He trod its waves that he might help the weary rowers when the wind was contrary. He woke from his sleep to still the tempest and save the affrighted men in whose ship he was crossing the sea. He rescued one sinking man. He filled the nets which the night's toiling had left empty. The first to hear the good news which he brought, and the first to tell it to the world, were sailors. The Lord himself leads us to the sea, directs our gaze to the wandering ships, bids us give to them as freely as we receive from him, teaches us that we can make them the messengers of his grace around the world.

What can we do for the seamen? We can place them in good ships, properly built and honestly loaded. That man has a title to royal distinction who has drawn around the ship the safety line which bears his name. We can give to them the protection of the law, that they may be fairly paid for their hazardous life, and that their earnings may be safe from the hands which would steal them. We can have our coast thoroughly surveyed, and its perils brought to light, that ships may go securely on their way. We can maintain lighthouses and lightships wherever they can be a warning and a guide. We can sustain our life-saving service, and let it do its work through all the year, seeing that storm and shipwreck cannot be regulated by the calendar.

We can give the sailors a home when they are on shore, and a friendly hand, and a genial companionship, which shall make their stay pleasant and safe. We can remember that to most of our seamen this is a foreign land, where they should receive from us the same attention which we are to provide for our own men when they are abroad. The sailor on shore, especially in a strange land, should find waiting for him a friend, a home, a church, a savings-bank, and whatever will supply his varied wants. We have but to think how greatly we are his debtor to be moved to repay him out of the abundance of our comfort.

We can put Bibles on every ship; a Bible for a

man. It is the book which he needs, even as we need it. The godliness which it teaches is profitable for his life, as it is for our own. God and his law, Christ and his redemption, the future and all which it contains, should be in his thoughts, and should be set there, kept there, enlarged there, by the Word which is a lamp and a light for men at sea and on shore. It is interesting to observe how much of the imagery of the Bible is drawn from the sea, and would naturally be most appreciated by seamen. Our days pass away as the swift ships. The virtuous woman is like the merchants' ships. The true hope in God is as an anchor of the soul. A man's life is influenced as great ships are turned about with a very small helm. "Deep calleth unto deep at the noise of thy waterspouts: all thy waves and thy billows are gone over me," cries the burdened and hopeful Psalmist. "When thou passest through the waters I will be with thee," is the Lord's promise. "When the enemy shall come in like a flood, the Spirit of the Lord shall lift up a standard against him." "The wicked are like the troubled sea, when it cannot rest." To the obedient his peace shall be as a river, and his righteousness as the waves of the sea. When St. John was a prisoner upon a rock in the midst of the sea, he saw the Son of Man in his glory, and his voice was as the sound of many waters; and the new song which he heard before the throne, the song of the redeemed from the earth, was in a voice "as the voice of many waters."

The hymn which so clearly expresses in melodious form the grace of the Saviour and the trust of the soul in him, among the dearest of all our Christian songs, carries our thoughts at once out upon the sea. It seems almost to have been written for sailors —

> Jesus, Lover of my soul,
>   Let me to thy bosom fly,
> While the waters near me roll,
>   While the tempest still is high:
> Hide me, O my Saviour, hide,
>   Till the storm of life is past;
> Safe into the haven guide :
>   Oh, receive my soul at last!

But we are able to give to the sailor other books. There is scarcely a limit to our ability in this direction. There are few good books which are read in our homes which would not be suitable on board the ship. In some respects a man has the advantage of a book as a companion and instructor. In other important respects the advantage is with the book. The book has its wit and wisdom in a condensed form. It is patient. It will tarry the sailor's leisure, and speak whenever he is disposed to listen. It will repeat its words as often as it is asked. It will not crowd him in his house, nor be in his way on deck. It will eat none of the ship's bread and demand none of its favors. The good book will be the good friend, suited to all climes, adapted to all the conditions of life. Like the sea-gull it will be at home in the calm, and will beat up against the gale.

This book we can furnish and ship in profusion and variety. Books of travel and history, of geography and biography, of science and art; stories which are worth reading; poetry which will be a delight; books which teach virtue and religion — one and the same book which we use and prize, which we buy for our homes and place in our public libraries — these we can give to those who go down to the sea in ships, away from public libraries, and book-stores, and newspapers, with the leisure of a long voyage, with the intervals between the storms, with the weary days when a new face, and a fresh voice, and a novel thought will be welcomed and cherished.

In the work of civilization, the man and the book go through the world together. We should keep them together when we can. There should be chaplains at all seaports. But we cannot provide twenty-five thousand chaplains that each of our ships may be furnished. They would not be received if we could provide the men. There is no difficulty in furnishing twenty-five thousand libraries, that each ship may have one. The American Seaman's Friend Society, through which our part of this work is to be done, has already sent out more than seventy-five hundred libraries, containing more than five hundred thousand volumes. It had placed at the last report nine hundred and thirty five libraries in the ships of the navy and in naval hospitals, and one at each of our life-saving stations. The work is as simple as it is sensible and useful. I have been told that it was a woman's thought, and I can readily believe it. Twenty dollars sends a library to sea; not on one voyage only, but on a series of voyages. It may be exchanged for another in some distant port, or on the high seas. It may return to be recruited, that it may again go abroad. For the price of a book you or I can go on this voyage of helpfulness, to be the sailor's companion and assistant, to cheer him in his loneliness, to shield him in his peril, to bind him to his home, to point him to the Father's house, and attend him on the upward way. It is an opportunity to be heartily seized. What work in which we engage promises so large a return for so small an outlay! So wide an influence with so little exertion! We can stay at home, and send our line out through all the earth, and our words to the end of the world. It is a magnificent enterprise, simple as it is. All which commends it to us as we think upon it is enhanced when we see the eagerness with which these books are sought, the care which they receive, the signs of faithful reading which they bring back from their wandering. It would be hard for a generous man to look upon a returned library, to take the books in his hand, to catch the aroma which is breathed out from the case and the books, and not desire to go upon a voyage so easily made, and to have a sailor's library for a part of his own life.

The results which have attended this unostentatious service confirm all which has been said. The testimony is abundant and continuous. Men have been cheered and helped. They have been protected when among enemies. They have been taught the way of righteousness. Many have become doers of the word of life, and confessing Christ as their Saviour have entered upon his service with heartiness and have been efficient laborers in his name. Sailors say that in coming around Cape Horn, or the Cape of Good Hope, the first land they make is the North Star. On many a sea and from many a ship sailors have seen the Star in the East which has led them to the place where the young child lay who was afterward to call men from their boats into his service.

There is a special significance in the Christian life of a sailor because he is a wanderer on the earth. He visits many lands where he can be the living witness to the power and principle of the truth which he teaches with his lips and illustrates in his life. Before Paganism and its vices he can show forth the better way of pure and undefiled religion. Himself a missionary, he can stay up the hands and strengthen the heart and enlarge the success of those who have gone into strange lands only that they might preach the unsearchable riches of Christ who loved them, and loved all men, and gave himself for the world.

For the special enterprise which we are considering to-day, we may draw incentive and example from other work which is done for seamen. Not for them alone, but for ourselves when we are sharing their perils. The government erects lighthouses and guards them with generous care. We can hold the lamp of life along the shore, and out on the sea, and in foreign ports, that men may reach the haven which they should desire. We can meet the sailor wherever he goes with the light of the world. We can make him a light to lighten the Gentiles. By his help we can make the world bright with the glory of God, and the Lamb shall be the light thereof. Our life-saving service is well named, and, while it is not yet perfected, is an honor to the land. Wonderful is the efficiency of its one hundred and six stations. Think of two thousand lives saved in a single year, and a million and a half dollars worth of property preserved. What work is grander and more humane than that which is done by the hardy and resolute men to whom this mercy is intrusted? It was not many months ago that men whose time was out and whose pay was stopped saved thirty passengers, with the sailors of the *Pliny*, which had presumed to be wrecked at the wrong season. A life-saving service which shall extend its watch and its labors to the souls of men, that they may not perish, but have everlasting life, is demanded by humanity and Christianity. It is organized. It needs more men and more money for its work. It appeals to every kind and noble impulse. The very luxuries on our table urge us to the payment of our debt to sailors. The books which we enjoy plead for liberty to go out and bless others. The storms of winter bear to our retreat the cry of the needy whose hold on life is frail. He whose friends we are bids us walk the sea after him, that we may do good.

I am sure that you will let a sailor's son plead with you in the sailors' behalf. I pray you to carry them in your hearts, to pray for them, to share with them the blessings which gladden your life — the blessings which have come to you through their hands. The opportunity is as inviting as it is large.

"We are as near to heaven by sea as by land," were the words of Sir Humphrey Gilbert as his bark entered the darkness of the night, to be seen no more. The way to heaven proves shorter than the way by land. Heaven is near to bless the wanderer with grace, to guide him with divine counsel that he may be received into glory. The promises of the Lord's kingdom include the sea. At last there shall be no more sea: no more will it part friend from friend. It will imperil no life. It will take no man into its dark depths. When the graves are opened, the great sepulchre will render up its dead, and roll away forever. Before that day the Lord will have his own. It is written, and it shall be fulfilled, that the abundance of the sea shall be converted unto him. Our faith and our work are to be as broad as the promise. When we pray and when we give, we should stand with one foot on the land and one foot on the sea, sure that when time shall be no more, the endless years shall still be ours; ours and theirs who are in our mind and on our heart to-day. With a long vision, with a controlling faith, with generous purposes, let us go up now and look toward the sea.

V.

THE GOOD MERCHANT.

IN MEMORY OF MR. JAMES P. MELLEDGE.

SCRIPTURE LESSON: *Romans,* xii.
TEXT : Happy is the man that findeth wisdom, and the man that getteth understanding.
For the merchandise of it is better than the merchandise of silver, and the gain thereof than fine gold.
She is more precious than rubies : and all the things thou canst desire are not to be compared unto her.
Length of days is in her right hand; and in her left hand riches and honor.
Her ways are ways of pleasantness, and all her paths are peace.
She is a tree of life to them that lay hold upon her: and happy is every one that retaineth her. *Proverbs* iii: 13-18.

THERE have been many among us who have found these sayings true, and have illustrated their truth before men. Of these some remain, honored and trusted, serving Christ and the Church, wearing meekly the homage which belongs to usefulness. Others have gone from us, entering into their rest, advancing in their reward, yet leaving with us blessed memories which we delight to cherish, and a gracious influence for which we give thanks at every thought of them. The life of a good man is a present and permanent good. It is helpful to the strong and the true. It is profitable to the weak and the wavering. It gives hope to the old, who are soon to intrust their work to other hands. It gives wisdom to the young, calling them to noble lives and quickening every manly endeavor. This is especially true when the life has been made up within the common bounds, and out of ordinary material, so that it can stand as a pattern for other lives. This is of the greater service if the life has been seen day by day, as deed has been joined to deed; where purpose and principle and effort and result could all be observed and intelligently considered. There is one thing which is evident, that the good life may be lived in any part of the world, in any age, with any outward estate, with any position among men. It is evident, also, that it can be engaged in any kind of honest work. The good man may be a prophet or apostle; he may be the minister of the Church, to teach the Gospel of the grace of God. He may be a lawyer, concerned with divine justice and righteousness as they are to be applied to the affairs of men for their guidance. He may be a physician, carrying the Gospel of God's healing into the homes of men, that their days may be prolonged in the earth. He may be a teacher opening the world of God's truth and order before the expectant eyes which wait for the revelation. He may be a mechanic, framing the wood and stone which God has made into houses and ships, that households may live in comfort, and climes exchange their products, and nations become neighbors. Our thoughts add another to the brief list. The good man may be a merchant. He may have to do with merchandise, with buying and selling, with finance and economy; standing between the earth and her children, in the name of the Lord, to bring out the treasures of the land and the sea, the forest and the mine, and lay them at the feet of those who need them. It is most appropriate to-day that in our study of a good life we keep a merchant in mind. Instructed by our recollection and affection we are certain to do this. We are glad and grateful that we can do it with an ample confidence. Yet no sooner do we seek thus to confine our thoughts than they reach away beyond the name we have chosen and the life which it describes. The good man may be a merchant, but he must be more. His business may be upon a vast scale, but his life must be more vast. He has relations and corresponding duties towards his father and mother, while they are here, and towards their home. If he has a family of his own, he has peculiar and sacred obligations towards those who bear his name and look to him for support and counsel. He has duties to the community with which he is connected, whose interests he must regard. Above all he must remember his Creator, and give to God reverent obedience and affection. He must make up a Christian career, true in doctrine, just in conduct, devoted in purpose, humane, charitable, beneficent.

Whatever be the special occupation by which a man is known, he has these broad relationships in which he must be found faithful. A good life is not a point, nor is it a line. It is a circle whose circumference encloses many different things, compassing them in a regular and unbroken curve. Herein lies the glory of manhood, that it is large and generous; that it is complete and right. Have I said more than we have seen in the lives of men? More than one name could be written underneath the picture; one name your tender thought has been speaking.

Look now more closely and more fully at some of the things which properly find a place in the life of a good merchant.

I. First, then, it is of great value to a man to be well born. One cannot secure this for himself. No man is forbidden to be great for the want of it; no man is assured of a noble life because of it. Yet happy is he who possesses it. Manhood descends. If character be personal, the forces which make up character are in a good measure inherited. It is the solemn law working grandly when the inheritance is grand. It enlarges human life. It makes it possible for a man to improve upon himself and to give to his sons a better start than was given to him. Working normally, it secures an advance by generations. The father and mother may give to their child disposition, taste, tendency, with opinions, motives, powers. The birthright is long in their keeping as the child's guardian, that he may have his own with usury, through their watchfulness, influence, training. This is according to the divine ordinance. The good parent, says an old English writer, "beginneth his care for his children at their birth, giving them to God to be, if not his chaplains, at least his servants. This care he continueth till the day of his death, in their infancy, youth, and man's estate." Manifestly it is a great advantage to a boy to have such parentage: to be born of those who have a complete view of life and a thorough conception of duty; to begin his career in a house where God is loved and served; to be brought up from his infancy in the knowledge of his other and greater Father: of his commandment, his providence, his mercy; and to have his spiritual nature trained for the years and the ages which are before it. It is a great help to a boy to have for his father an honest man: upright, frugal, industrious: whose days of strength are given to profitable work, and whose riper years are hallowed with an active charity; to grow up in a house whose hospitality finds its most frequent guest in a godly man, an angel entertained not unawares: a disciple lodged for the Master's sake.

> Be his
> My special thanks, whose even-balanced soul,
> From first youth tested up to extreme old age,
> Business could not make dull, nor passion wild;
> Who saw life steadily, and saw it whole.

With such parents, in such a home, a boy may be spirited, fond of adventure, full of enterprise; a leader in the heroic sports of youth. He may be quiet, content with home and school, marked in his work and play by gentleness and courtesy. Either boy may be truthful, reverent, manly, and give promise of a creditable life. I have in mind to-day the quiet, courteous boy; whose ardor was tempered with gentleness; whose strength rejoiced in beauty of spirit and behavior. What will the man be out of this beginning?

II. In answering this I remark, secondly, that it belongs to the good merchant to have a wise choice of his calling. Not all good men are suited to one method of life. One spirit may be in them all, while they have diversities of gifts which should find diversities of operations. It would not have been strange if from the associations of his boyhood this young man had chosen to be a minister, and doubtless he would have been wise as a winner of souls. With his kind heart and careful hands he would probably have been a skilful physician. In either profession he would have found a wide field for goodness and strength.

It was most natural that he should choose his father's calling: and the result has justified the choice. What department of business should he select? Brought up by an established mercantile house, he turned from that special kind of business to another which offered to the young merchant an opening into a free and remunerative service. He chose that for which he was fitted: therefore he chose well. Yet making a wise selection of a career is but one part of the good merchant's choice. He must also determine what manner of man he will be in his work. Some things seem settled for him. According to his temperament and education, he may be stirring, enterprising, pushing into new countries, finding strange avenues for trade; or he may mingle great prudence with his zeal, regard new enterprises with caution, and let his diligence satisfy itself in paths where he is familiar with the way. This man was zealous and careful: diligent and wise. Whatever his character in this respect, he has to choose in what way he will regard his business; whether it shall be for narrow or broad results; whether it shall be content with temporal or seek, also, eternal reward; whether it shall be of the earth earthy, or be in its intent spiritual like himself; whether his business shall be master of him, or he shall be the master; whether he shall follow the maxims of the world, or work under the commandment of God. One may be a merchant on either plan. The good merchant will elect the better plan. He will dignify his business with the lofty temper which he takes into it. He will make it the means of his spiritual culture. He will order it after his own will, under the statutes beneath which he lives. Realizing how large a part of his time and strength he is giving to his business, he will make sure that he is not separating so much of his life from its chief end and worthy method. He will refuse to divide his manhood according to days or places. He will be himself because in himself he is at his best. A man divided is like a house divided. The best everywhere, will be his rule. The merchandise of wisdom "is better than the merchandise of silver, and the gain thereof than fine gold!" Therefore he will get wisdom and not sell it. He will work in "a land whose stones are iron and out of whose hills thou mayest dig silver." In his daily life, in all its common concerns, he will keep his integrity, and preserve the graces of his character and manners, carrying "high erected thoughts seated in the heart of courtesy." I will conclude and adorn this account with words written more than two hundred years ago —"The good merchant is one who, by his trading, claspeth the islands to the continent, and one country to another; an excellent gardener who makes England bear wine, and oil, and spices; yea, herein goes beyond nature in causing that *omnis fert omnia tellus*. He wrongs not the buyer in number, weight, or measure. These are the landmarks of all trading, which must not be removed. God is the principal clerk of the market; "all the weights of the bag are his work!" Sometimes "the seller's conscience is all the buyer's skill." Men have a touchstone whereby to try gold; but gold is the touchstone whereby to try men." And this is fitting here: " The true gentleman " "is courteous and affable to his neighbors. As the sword of the best tempered metal is most flexible, so the truly generous are most pliant and courteous in their behavior to their inferiors." Is all this true of the merchant who is most in our minds? Is it not true? What honor it is thus to have borne himself honorably, trusty in his calling, faithful to himself, always remembering that before he was a merchant he was a man : and that when he should cease to be a merchant, he would still be a man! To hold this in his thought was to make his work prosperous, and his gains lasting. This enlarges courage, lengthens patience, and uplifts the life. It increases and improves the man. He needs to let his best assert itself. He is more than his powers, and more than his life. He is spirit. Eternal years are on him. This true and abiding nature, *the real man*, wins or loses life. A man's treasure is his character. If that is rich, he is rich. He is so much that he can be more; so high that he can be higher.

He can be good, and have his goodness solid and round. I wish to pay this grateful tribute to the men who make us all their debtors, as they keep society alive, uphold government, found schools, build churches, send missionaries through the lands. I have revered them as boy and man, and lived upon their bounty. I know how great their own rules would make them, if they would take their rules into the limitless years and along the uppermost walks of life.

> Still doth the soul, from its lone fastness high,
> Upon our life a ruling effluence send;
> And when it fails, fight as we will, we die,
> And while it lasts, we cannot wholly end.

III. This leads me to remark, thirdly, that the good merchant will be good towards God. He may be a merchant without this; honest and honorable, strong and wealthy. But surely these are not the highest things to be said of a man. The merchant can surpass all this. Seeing that he is wrong with God, he will become right; confessing the wrong, seeking forgiveness, praying for strength to do those things which are pleasing in his sight. The qualities which make the merchant successful in the esteem of men, if carried to their proper end, will make him great in goodness. The wise merchant looks before him and as far he can. He does not bound his vision by seventy days; nor does he stop at seventy years if he can see beyond —and he can see beyond. Indeed, the years after the threescore and ten are more certain than those upon this side. He is a man of faith. He confides in men, enters upon projects in which absolute certainty is impossible; he sends his ships beyond his sight; invests money for a future return; anticipates results and works with his expectations. He should not be kept from a godly life because he does not know everything about it, and has never seen the Lord face to face Nor should he refuse to heed the teachings of God because in part they concern unseen things and reach into the world beyond the earth. He should pass on from what he knows to what he ought to know, and let his reason have free course. He is an honorable man; dealing fairly by all, paying that which he ought to pay, meeting men in a liberal and manly spirit. The same sense of honor will make him just towards God, desirous to meet his duties to him, carrying himself in a manful and becoming manner towards his Creator and his Father. It is most becoming that he should be a man of God in a large and generous way. The wise merchant seeks the best, or that which is best for his purposes, and shrewdly conducts his business with reference to the largest gains. He should not stop when the gain becomes very large and the good things perfect. Religion in itself, and its return, "is more precious than rubies," said a man who knew something both of rubies and religion; "and all the things thou canst desire are not to be compared unto her." Our Lord himself sought to extend the approved methods of business, and he taught men how far they reach. "The kingdom of heaven is like unto a merchantman seeking goodly pearls; who, when he had found one pearl of great price, went and sold all that he had, and bought it." The wise merchant is an economist. He does not work for pleasure, but for gain. From loss he turns away. Hence the question of the Gospel appeals to him and impresses him; a question profound enough for him, and simple enough for his office boy, "What shall it profit a man if he shall gain the whole world and lose his own soul? or what shall a man give in exchange for his soul?" He seeks moreover for permanence. He prides himself on the stability of his business — "an old established house," he likes to say. So that he can appreciate the force of Christ's appeal; "Whosoever heareth these sayings of mine, and doeth them, I will liken him unto a wise man, which built his house upon a rock." The shrewd merchant makes himself known; chooses a place among men, puts up his sign, advertises his goods, lets himself be recognized by buyers and sellers, by producers and consumers, as one engaged in his line of trade. Hence he will approve the command of Christ, that the Christian shall let his light so shine before men that the light may produce the best effect. He knows the advantage of association for counsel and helpfulness; he has his Exchange and his Board of Trade, to which he gives, from which he seeks. He sees therefore the wisdom of Christ in bringing Christians together in the fellowship of the Church for the furtherance of the Christian design and for the advantage of all.

With what force, then, does Christ address himself to the wise merchant, when he asks him to extend his practical maxims and usages, and let his wisdom carry him as far as it can. This merchant who is with us to-day looked very far before him; he saw the invisible; he cherished a sense of honor which brought him to God; he strove to do his duty before him, that God might be glorified; walking with God, he sought to secure the highest and most permanent gains, and what he received was still the Lord's. More than this, he knew his weakness, his failures, his faults. In a simple truthfulness he confessed his sins and sought the mercy of his God. To the Lord who had redeemed him, he gave his life. Two and thirty years old, he stood before men in the Church and made confession of his Lord and Saviour, and joined himself to others of like character and purpose. He sought what the Church had to give.

He gave what the Church sought and he had to give. His piety was real; more, it was effective. It owed much of its effectiveness to the fact that it was known. He opened his mouth and quietly said, "I am a Christian." Therefore the good which he did and the good which he was became a tribute to his Lord. Men thought better of Christ and the Church because he had told them that he was following Christ, and they saw that he was in the Church and of it. This was the business man carrying his business habits further on. This was the wise merchant become the good merchant.

IV. I add, therefore, fourthly, that the good merchant will make for himself a Christian life. It will be long, stretching down the centuries, and it will begin here. It will be a life of obedience. The eternal rules of righteousness will be its law. The Lord will be its master. He will realize that he has no more power over right and wrong than he has over the life which rustles in his grain, or the winds which drive his ships across the sea. He will no more tamper with the laws of God than with the coin of the realm. It is for him to obey. He will do this cheerfully, because he knows that it is right, and that the rule of Christ is the rule of the best. Thus honor and honesty are secure. He will be conservative towards the eternal right. Methods of business may change, steam and lightning may become factors in it, its competitions may grow more fierce, its demands more extortionate. But in his mind truth will remain truth; right, right; honor, honor. Novelty may play upon the surface of his business; underneath will be the old vigorous rules of righteousness.

Thus he will have a life of purity. His conscience will sit at his desk and stand by his scales. His mother might be his active partner and his father audit his acounts. He will be orderly and accurate: intelligent and sound. This will give him calmness. He may be full of enterprise, but he will behave as a man who has himself well in hand, and is prepared against surprises. He will enjoy the quiet

> Of toil unsevered from tranquility;
> Of labor, that in lasting fruit outgrows
> Far noisier schemes, accomplish'd in repose,
> Too great for haste, too high for rivalry.

Such a life must be generous. It will be put to the proof. Its patience will be tried, its passion tested. Forbearance and charity will often be needed. Broad opportunities of usefulness will open on every hand. Many claimants will ask a share of his gains. He will need all his discretion. But he will know that business is not an end unto itself, and that the value of money is in that which can be done with it. He will give by principle and with a free hand. The main course of his life will be for the common good. But many subordinate interests will also be regarded. He will sow his rich fields for the large harvest; and from his overflowing hand some seed will fall at the wayside for the birds.

Under such training, wherein he trains himself, he will increase in goodness. His life will rise as it lengthens. He will grow into the image of his Redeemer, and his Lord, and share his life. Wisdom will endow him. For "length of days is in her right hand; and in her left hand riches and honor." He will enjoy life. For "her ways are ways of pleasantness, and all her paths are peace." He will increase in strength. For "she is a tree of life to all that lay hold upon her." He will be received on high when he goes hence. "For whosoever shall confess me before men, him will I also confess before my Father which is in heaven." Is the picture which my unskilful hand has drawn, and embellished with touches from the king's fingers, — is it like the man?

Obedient, the law of the Lord was his law, and the statutes of God were his song. He learned obedience in his boyhood; and with it he made his manhood strong. His was the soul of honor. His nature was large and his principles were free, but you knew where you would find him. He loved truth the better because it was old, and ancestral piety was dear to him. What we call conservatism, it is better in him to call truthfulness: loyalty to the right — the unalterable right. He was one man. He had his house, his business, his society; but he was the same man in all: the Christian gentleman. He planned a full life, and went on to construct it. The centre was Christ: the circle held his children, his neighbors, his associates and the Church. He said not over much; but what he said was with power from the man behind it. He spoke often enough to make men sure that he was a Christian, then he went forward with Christian deeds. Nature had been generous, but the man had been just. There was more than nature in his calmness and courtesy. Let us do credit to his conscience and his will. The winds passed over him as over other men, and sometimes the sea was rough. Yet he went steadily on and safely. There was a man in the ship. One of our New England writers has remarked, " When I see a man with serene countenance, it looks like a great leisure that he enjoys; but in reality he sails on no summer's sea. This steady sailing comes of a heavy hand on the tiller." There was deliberation in his life. He knew what he would do and how he meant to do it. A calm assurance of substantial things made him firm and robust. The results are in keeping with the design. Given such purposes and principles, and the life is the natural consequence. He illustrates what another has written : " Sow an act, and you reap a habit.

Sow a habit, and you reap a character. Sow a character, and you reap a destiny."

But the divine part of this life is its distinctive feature. Once more let us assert it. This man was born of God. The author of his faith and charity is divine. He knew his Father. He loved him. He delighted to please him. His Father delighted in him and advanced him in wisdom and honor. " Happy is the man that findeth wisdom, and the man that getteth understanding ; " " That friend of mine who lives in God."

He trusted in the grace of God. He bowed at the manger with his gold and frankincense. He knelt at the cross with his penitence and faith. He stood at the open sepulchre with his love and his life. He received the Holy Ghost, the Comforter. He walked with Christ and went prepared unto the place prepared. Therefore while we are sad, the voice from out the skies is saying, ' Blessed " — " Blessed are the dead which die in the Lord." For they are not dead ; " they rest." They have not parted from their business ; " their works do follow them." We speak our loving praise. We whisper our lament. We strain our eyes to look up the glittering path and through the radiant door into the brightness and blessedness which are forever. There are glory and honor and immortality.

There they stand, true men who have gone up from the earth, and they are pillars in the temple of God. They behold their Lord and are like him, for they see him as he is.

> Saints in glory, we together,
> Know the song that ceases never;
> Song of songs, Thou art, O Saviour,
>   All that endless day.
>
> O the unsearchable Redeemer!
> Shoreless Ocean, sounded never!
> Yesterday, to-day, forever,
>   Jesus Christ, the same!

VI.

WHY STAND YE GAZING?

SCRIPTURE LESSON: *Revelation* i.
TEXT: Why stand ye gazing up into heaven? *Acts* i : 2.

THE answer was obvious. These men had come from Jerusalem to the mount called Olivet, with one who had led them all the way, and who, while he was talking with them, stretched his hands over them in blessing, and while he blessed them, suddenly rose from the ground and ascended until a cloud received him out of their sight. They gazed after him as long as they could see him; and when he had vanished, naturally their eyes remained fixed upon the cloud into which he had entered. "Why stand ye gazing up into heaven?" One would think that the angel who asked the question might have allowed them a few minutes of rapturous longing as they looked after him who was more than all the world to them. Yet it seems, when we read the New Testament, as if it were not meant that the disciples should enjoy these rare visions. Three of these men had gone up a mountain at the north, led by the same One, and a glory exceeding bright had shone around about him, and there had come two men in the glory to talk with him. The disciples at last were brought to the very gate of heaven. It was worth while to be a disciple if this could be the reward. While they looked and enjoyed, and desired that they might build three tents and remain there, suddenly a cloud shut out the whole vision from their gaze; they heard a voice speaking out of the cloud; they fell upon their faces afraid, and presently they were led down out of the brightness into the darkness and misery of the world. Does it mean that God will not let us see the glory before the time? Does it mean that heaven is fearful lest we should have too much of its delight while we possess the earth which is now our dwelling-place?

Angels hold men to their place and work. When the women come to anoint the Lord with spices and embalm him with the last act of their devotion for his long slumber, looking forward out of the sorrow of the night to the few moments which they might have with him in the sacred solitude of the garden, before they began the holy offices which they were to perform, angels interrupted the course of their loving thoughts — " Why seek ye the living among the dead? Go quickly, and tell his disciples that he is risen from the dead." Truly, there were surrounding the friends of our Lord the guardian angels of God's presence, coming to them from time to time to help them, certainly coming to them when there was much danger that they would be unduly exalted and forget that they belonged in this world, that their life was here, that they were to look down into the wants of the world, and to do the work which God had given them. Perhaps we find in this coming, more than anywhere else, the meaning of that phrase which is so familiar to our thoughts and so precious in our hopes, "ministering spirits."

When these men come down from the Mount, they are not the men who went up. They are not so rich, it may be said, for they have lost their great teacher, their leader, their master. They are richer, it were better to say, because he who was their Lord has gone up on high, and has taken to himself his greater power. Life never can be the same to them again, because one who is their life has gone to his own place, a place full of blessedness and of life. To have one's best friend in heaven sanctifies the earth. To have one's Lord at the throne makes it easier to obey here. To have the Intercessor there makes it easier to pray here. To have one there who is able to give the Comforter to men makes it easier to bear the trouble of this life, and to strengthen ourselves for the service which is required at our hands.

These disciples needed to be instructed in the meaning of the ascension of the Lord. "Why stand ye gazing" recalled them to the true significance of this act which consummates our Lord's earthly life. It was the gaze of wonder; they were surprised that he had gone up. Let them remember that he had just said, "I am to ascend." "I ascend unto my Father and your Father, and to my God and your God." It was the look of bereavement; yet it need not have been. Rather it should have been one of gladness to find that Christ had gone out of his humiliation into his glory. They should have recalled his word of promise, that he would be with his disciples, even unto the end of the world; and that other word, that he would give the Holy Spirit to abide with men even while they were in this world. It was a look of longing; they wanted him back again. There was that strange confusion of faith and desire which is so common; which makes us long with a longing that cannot be expressed for the presence, for the voice, of those who have gone out of our sight; yet makes us give thanks every morning and night for the rest and the bliss which have come to them. The desire of these disciples changes into confidence when they recall the promise of the Lord as it is repeated by the angel: "This same Jesus which is taken up from you into heaven, shall so come in like manner as ye have seen him go into heaven."

This would almost seem a reason why the men should stand gazing up into heaven, watching for his return. What is the reason, then, of this interruption? Why are they not allowed to look up into the place out of which their Lord shall presently come? Because the Lord is not to come presently. One day is as a thousand years with him, and a thousand years are as one day. They are not able to stand waiting and looking until he shall come. Physical necessities, the very weariness of their bodies, the very hunger which would oppress them, must soon draw their gaze down from the clouds and send them back into the world. They are not able to stay upon the mountain; let them come down, not of necessity, but of their own will.

Again, they are not to stand gazing up into heaven, because the work which they are to do lies not in heaven, but below them, in the world. These facts which have entered into their experience have been given that they might become the possession of the world. It is interesting to see how often the smallest causes which work in our life move hand in hand with the greatest causes and the highest obligations which enter into our career. Common hunger and vulgar weariness would send men from the mountain into the world, and the command of Christ, with the grandest commission ever given to men, would have the same result. It recalls to mind, although it is not strictly analogous, that it was out of the necessities of men that Christ wrought his great works of mercy. He fed the multitudes by divine power because they were hungry; and the need of men as really worked for their relief as the power of God. He raised men from the dead because they were dead; and the death of men became one of the forces as really as the power which called them from their long sleep. So here, the common duties and wants of men, which would carry them back into the world in which they belonged, would work together with that command of Christ which was their commission and the warrant of their discipleship.

The sight of their ascending Lord would strengthen his disciples for their work, his work. It has been often seen that, when God has called men to great service, he has given them a vision of himself and let them hear his voice. He spoke to Moses out of the bush, and to Paul at the gate of Damascus. He has given men a sight of his glory, that they might glorify the world with the special revelation which had been made to them.

Let us mark, then, the order of service; for it is of importance that we preserve it. We look upon the disciples as exceptional men, with an exceptional work. We scarcely dare to think of their work or experience as like our own. They had marvellous revelations, and a remarkable furnishing. But they received power in connection with certain grand facts which were to be the strength of their lives. In this how far below them do we stand? For we have the same facts and the same

Holy Spirit. It is to be noted that much of the strength with which Christ furnishes men is the power of external facts, with which they have nothing to do as causing them, or deserving them, or expecting them; but certain great verities which are wrought out by God, and which they are to take, and by means of them make their will, their conscience, and their life strong and efficient. Thus, if you take this fact of our Lord's ascension, it becomes a power in these men's lives, because they think of the glory of him who has gone; and it gives a wonderful authority to his words; it gives a new force to the love which they have for him. Everything which he did is magnified before them by this glory, which sheds its brightness upon his whole life. For we join with this all our Lord's life. His ascension is simply one in a series of facts. It does not seem the most important; yet it is important as belonging to a system of events, beginning with the incarnation, running through the display of his divine power in miracle, and quite as much in his instruction and promise, including the height and depth of divine grace when he gave himself in sacrifice and entered the sepulchre, to come forth in power when he burst the bands of death and the grave, and stood alive among men; taking us at last to the Mount of Olives, when he rises into the clouds of heaven.

These are not things which we have done, or which God accomplishes within our heart; they are things which God works outside of us — out of doors, if I may say so — things which we are to look upon and to take as the material out of which we are to build up our thought and life. It is to be to us a verity that Christ rose from the dead, and that verity is to control our life; it is to become a part of our mind, and of our moral faculties; it is to enter into our reason; it is to touch our hands, and our feet, and our lips; and we are to be different in the commonest things which we do, from the fact that Christ died for us and rose from the dead.

In this way God instructs men. For the work of the disciples, it may not seem to be essential that they should see Christ mount into the clouds of heaven. But it was essential that they should see him, and that all the fabric of their thought and life should be affected by that fact. They might, indeed, repeat the story of Christ's life; they might tell of his miracles; they might renew his teachings among men; they might be honest and truthful, and fill up the measure of a good man's career in the world; but the life which they were to live, the work which they were to do, they could not live and they could not do, except as these facts entered into their thoughts, and were absorbed into their feeling, that Christ had ascended into his glory; that Christ had risen from the dead; that Christ had died for them; that Christ had become incarnate for them. It is impossible that these things should become a part of the staple of any man's life, and the whole life not be affected, and elevated, and the man strengthened to live by the power of these divine truths.

This was the method of our Lord's instruction to men. Certainly so much as this was true, that he was not satisfied to teach them merely with the word of his lips or by an inspiration in their minds. He taught them, as he teaches you and me, by events. Hence he let them behold his incarnation; he let them see divine power raising the dead; he let them see him coming forth out of the sepulchre alive; he let them, with their own eyes, see him ascend into the clouds of heaven; that, taking these things, they might out of them learn who he was and why he was here, and what it was to be his disciples, and what the gift was which he gave to them and which through them he was to give to the world.

We stand related to these facts precisely as the disciples stood. We stand in the same place. We stand in that interval of God's providence which has not been closed since the day of Christ's ascension; that period which was often described by our Lord, and in many different ways, as the time between his vanishing from the world and his returning to the world; an interval wherein we are to take these things of Christ and to use them for the world's good. The question which the angels asked of the disciples on the mount of the

Ascension, and which I have brought to your notice this morning, reminds us that it is not enough for any man to gaze at these facts; it is not enough for us to believe them, to think about them, to enjoy them. It is not enough in our common work for a man to gaze at his store, to gaze at the opportunities which are before him, at the books which he might read, and the world which he might study, and the duties which he might perform. All this comes to nothing, and we weary of the dreamers, the visionary men who have a great prospect of something to which they never attain, and who, stirred by vain hopes, are unwilling to put their hands to the common things which lie at their feet. We say to a man — and how often and how truly we say it — you will never do the distant thing until you do the near; you never will attain unto the upper glory unless you are willing to stand here upon this common rough, and rugged earth, and do the first duty, and on that first duty mount to something higher. Gazing at duty and dreaming and singing and hoping and believing, all come to nothing, unless one puts his hand to the work and takes up, in substantial earnest, that which God has given him to do. There come times in life when success depends not only upon the recognition of this principle, but upon the speedy apprehension of it. There are men who work out their success — and perhaps all men work out their success in this way who have it at all — by a certain ability, which is almost genius, to recognize the right thing to do; the facts which they are to take into their life; and then quickly to take them up. I almost think you could describe the difference between a successful man and an unsuccessful man at that single point. The successful man is a man who does not gaze, but who does. Still, that does not quite closely enough define him. I should say that the successful man is a man who not only does, but does quickly. He makes up his mind readily; and having once made it up, he cleaves to his purpose, not gazing back, wishing he had made another choice, but keeping to that which he has made with a certain dogged perseverance which fastens the whole force of his hands and of his heart upon his work, and leaves him no leisure for idle dreaming or useless regrets.

One of the shrewdest business men I ever knew told me that when a transaction had passed out of his hands, though it might appear that he had lost by the method in which he had made it, he never mourned over it, or wished that he had waited another day; he simply accepted it as a fact behind him which it was of no profit for him to gaze upon, and went on to make up in to-day and to-morrow for the losses of yesterday. It is a wise principle, not to gaze backwards and wish we had done something else, not to gaze forward and wish we had something else, but to put ourselves in this interval where we stand to the doing of that which is our present duty.

The present duty of men is to do the will of God; and the will of God comes to us, not in a voice out of heaven merely; not in a voice from our own hearts merely; but the will of God comes to us in resounding syllables which every man can read. You can make out the letters one by one until you have the word; and these are the letters of the will of God which men are to hear and which men are to do to-day: "Incarnation," "Life," "Death," "Resurrection," "Ascension;" and these letters spell out the divine thought and the everlasting purpose of every truly successful man. But it will not serve us to gaze at these things; to wonder at the glories of the manger and where it was; to cross the seas that we may place our devotion in the sepulchre which we cannot find. But we are to take the facts and to do our business in the power of them; to carry the resurrection of Christ into our daily work; to take the ascension of Christ down into our studying and housekeeping, and all which engages our life, until we make up our thoughts and our purposes with these stupendous and divine factors which are the everlasting verities.

No man has made himself strong for his work who has not looked up into the heavens; and no man has looked up into the heavens to much purpose who has not come down from his gazing to his work in this world. We are permitted to see the risen Christ and to believe in him; and then, believing him, to follow him.

If you read the Lord's parables, you will find that again and again he refers to this interval in which we are living. Look, for instance, at his parable of the talents, or the parable of the pounds. A certain man takes his money and calls his servants, and talks with them concerning it; he puts the money into their hands, and goes into a far country to return. They know he is to return; they understand that his money is to be used. Perhaps they watch his receding form, and stare after him when he is lost to sight. They wonder where he has gone, and when he will come back, and they go home to talk about his goodness and kindness, and they turn the money over and over. Presently they begin to sing songs to this absent friend; to praise him, the most generous of all men. One man, finally, taking his pound which is so precious, wraps it in a napkin that no harm may come to it, and that it may be ready when the Lord shall return. Another, fearful of such security, digs a hole in the ground and buries his money, that it may be safe when the Lord comes back. Is that the way to watch for the coming of the Lord? Is that the meaning of this trust of talents and of pounds?

But what are the talents and the pounds? The opportunities of life, the privileges of life; our time and our ability. Yes, but there are other treasures. The real talents and the real pounds are these : The incarnation of God; the crucifixion of Christ; the resurrection of Christ; the ascension of Christ; the coming of the Holy Ghost to take of the things of Christ and show them unto us. These are talents and pounds which we are to use until the Lord comes back to reckon with us. Have we nothing to show him in that day but a little more character which we have gained, a little more influence we have acquired? He may well ask, " What have you done with my resurrection? Is that truth larger by that which you have done with it? Show me where my resurrection has gone down into your study and pervaded it. Show me where my ascension has entered into your thoughts and borne them up to higher and holier things."

So it was when the lord planted a vineyard and let it out to husbandmen, and went his way into a far country to receive for himself a kingdom and to return. It was a fine vineyard. He had built a tower in it, and a wine-press; he had prepared everything for the vintage. Then he went his way. There were the husbandmen with his interests in their charge. Had they nothing to do but to walk to and fro and see what a beautiful vineyard it was; to comment upon the architecture of the tower and the nature of its foundation ; to form elaborate calculations how long it would last, and how many men would probably be killed if it should fall? To speculate upon the prospect of fruitage if the men did nothing but trust to the sun and rain? Is that the way in which the husbandmen are to use the vineyard? They do so, I know. Such a method has high practical commendation. There are many men who seem to be doing nothing in God's vineyard except to admire it and to theorize upon it. Surely, the wise husbandmen are those who use the grounds, enlarge the quantity of the grapes, and bring forth the wine in its season. This is the preparation for the owner; not the gazing, but the doing. What is the vineyard to-day? What is it we are to do? We are to be more prudent and industrious; we are to study harder; we are to elevate our thought, and to be more rational and conscientious — certainly we are to do these things. But will men bring forth the abounding fruits of the vineyard by that process? Nay; the powers by which we are to do the work in the vineyard until the Lord comes, are such truths as I have named: Christ's life among men; Christ's redemption of men; his resurrection and his ascension. If we work these into our thoughts, and into our motives, and into our lives, by and by the heavy clusters shall hang upon the vine, and the Lord of the vineyard returning, shall greet us with his "good and faithful."

I want to present this to you to-day, and to my

own heart, as a lesson of encouragement. Life is too hard for any man to make it harder than is necessary; and the duties which are upon us are too exacting for any man to try to do them with insufficient strength and imperfect appliances. We are not asked to make up a Christian life in our own strength, or in the strength of the Church. God is better than that. He gives us the very presence of himself in the world, that we may be Christians; he gives us the very redemption of his Son; he grants us the resurrection of his Son and his ascension — the divinest powers which ever wrought in the universe, so far as we have any knowledge — to the end that we may be God's children, and may do the work of God. I pray you to see, that as long as we stand gazing at these things they do us very little good. There are, I suppose, men who make a merit of believing that Christ rose from the dead: they might as well make a merit of believing in the transit of Venus. It is of small consequence whether you believe that Christ rose from the dead or not, unless you take that fact down into your heart; take it into your will and make your will stronger by it; take it into your life and live by it from day to day. It is only as the resurrection becomes a power within our own power that it works out within us the peaceable fruits of God's purposes in man's righteousness.

This is what the world needs of us, brethren.

It is what we need, first of all, to receive these truths into our own thought and life, penitently, humbly, obediently; to receive the risen and ascended Christ as our Lord and our Saviour; to take strong and personal hold upon the divine and everlasting verities of his life, and then in the power of them, to go forth and do our work. I say this is what the world wants at our hands. So far as I can see, it is almost the only thing the world needs very much. I fail to see anything that the world wants to-day, which is any great necessity compared with its need of these truths which God gave to men that they might be God's men. You can give the world the benefit of your study; you can add the result of your invention and discovery; you can give your industry and the service of your daily life; and undoubtedly all that would do good. But there are many men doing the same thing, and there always will be. The world is not very poor from lack of learning to-day; nor from lack of mechanics, and merchants, and professional men of all kinds. It is not a very great gift to the world when one gives to it another commonplace and earthly life. The great thing the world wants, again, is not a change in our mechanism; new appliances, new organizations in the Church and in society; new methods which shall be filled with more energy. I grant that all these things may do good — I would not underrate them; but they never can do the grand work. The world can roll on quite well without them. The great thing the world wants to-day is the resurrection of Christ as a power in our streets, in our homes, and in all our work. It needs the glory of the ascension of Christ, until men trade with a bright cloud over their heads. We are to bear the troubles of life and indulge in its hopes, and live and die, carried up and carried forward on the wings of these grand realities, saying, "I have a Saviour, I have a Lord, who bears me on his heart before the throne of God; who is my keeper, my shepherd, and who presently, in an hour when I may not think of it, shall come to ask what I have done with the talent of the Resurrection, with the pound of the Ascension; what I have done in the vineyard which he planted with a cross."

Brethren, if I speak of what the world wants, may I not speak also of what heaven wants? Heaven seems to need such men as Christ would make. It is a mistake to suppose that heaven needs to be peopled. We cannot count the multitudes of it. Heaven needs but one thing: it needs those who are prepared for it. Heaven must be inhabited by men within whom there is incarnate the ascension of Christ; who have made up their lives around the truth that Christ died for them and rose and ascended; a truth which in the hands of the Holy Spirit takes away sin and breaks the power of the world, and renews and sanctifies and glorifies the heart. We overestimate ourselves if we think heaven will be impoverished without us. Still heaven wants us, and at our best; and no man is at his best until he has made up his character with the divine truths.

These things come to us in this world where we have need of them. It doubtless is true that we need them here as much as anywhere. It is in this world that these things have been wrought out, and that means that it is in this world they are to be used. Christ did not rise and ascend in heaven; he rose and ascended here. They make an earthly fact, an every-day truth. They furnish one of the commonplaces of God's government for this commonplace world. Let us take the facts here; then let us consent to the discipline of the world while they come to help us; to be a part of our training in patience, in charity, in faith, in all devotion. I know it seems hard to wait for the glory of the Lord; but the marble may well be content to tarry in the studio of the sculptor until he has touched it again and again; and the statue will be willing to wait, if it knows that presently the last rough and the final tender touch shall be given, and after that — not always kept under the chisel and the hammer; not always in this rude workshop, with the broken stone and scattered dust upon the floor; not always waiting among these masks and models — presently it shall stand out in its place of honor, where men shall look up to catch the thought that is incarnate in the marble, and the lips shall speak and the face shall reflect the thought of Him out of whom the creation has sprung; a living thought for a world that needs to be made alive.

Why stand we gazing into heaven? Let us take the truths of heaven and go down and live them out. The Lord is gone, but he is here. It is not the repeating of his name, it is the doing of his will which is to avail. He is here; not in the far country alone, but watching us here. When McGregor led his clan into the battle of Prestonpans, and the chief was wounded and fell bleeding upon the ground, his men, dismayed and disheartened, began to waver, until the wounded chieftain, raising himself upon his elbow, while the blood flowed from his wounds, cried out, "I am not dead, my children; I am looking at you, to see you do your duty." They rallied and rushed on to that whereunto he had called them to the field. Christ lives. He is here; he is looking at us. He is here, not to be met with our wondering eyes, but with our obedient life. "Blessed is that servant whom his Lord, when he cometh, shall find so doing." "He that doeth the will of God abideth forever."

> If any man will serve,
>   Then let him follow me;
> For where I am, be thou right sure,
>   There shall my servant be.

VII.

NOT BY MIGHT, BUT BY SPIRIT.

SCRIPTURE LESSON: 1 *Cor*. ii.
TEXT: Not by might nor by power, but by my spirit, saith the Lord of hosts. *Zech*. iv : 6.

THIS was one of the instances in which might and power, that is, a control by force, would be thought to have its place. It was a question between two nations, two peoples. The Jews had been trying for a long time to rebuild their temple. They had been carried into captivity. To gain the right to rebuild the temple would be the occasion for revolt. Let them conquer their oppressors, go back to their own country, and raise again the house which had been destroyed. But the record of the rebuilding is this: "The Lord stirred up the spirit of Cyrus." Cyrus was a Pagan and cared nothing for the temple; but the Lord stirred up his spirit to incite the Jews to build their house, and they began it. Then came those long periods of opposition, when Ahasuerus and Artaxerxes occupied the throne of Persia, and the Samaritans were continually hindering these temple-builders.

That was a time for them to rise against the Samaritans; it was a time for God to make bare his arm, as he had done against Pharaoh and his host. Instead of that, the Lord put it into the heart of Darius, the king, to search the records of the kingdom, where he found the old decree which God had inclined Cyrus to make. Renewing that decree, he rebuked the Samaritans, and required them to aid those whom they had been opposing. The temple rose to its completion, not by the might of arms, not by the power of revolution, but "by my spirit, saith the Lord of hosts." It became, then, in the highest sense, a house that was not made with hands.

This is to be accepted as God's ordinary way of working in the world. He does exercise power; he does come with judgment; he does put forth his omnipotent force and control men and nations; but his common way is quiet and gentle, in the hearts of men; and when he uses more violent and evident methods, in them and after them may be found this silent working of his spirit. The wind rends the mountains and breaks the rocks in pieces; the earthquake makes the hills tremble; the fire flashes from cliff to cliff, and lights the deep gorges; but God is not in wind, or earthquake, or fire. He comes "not by might, nor by power." But there is "after the fire a still, small voice."

This method of God's working commends itself to us. It is more majestic; it is grander. The

great forces of God work quietly, as in light and
life. It is more rational; it is the recognition of
God's spiritual nature and of man's, and of that
liberty which God has given to man so that he is
not to be compelled, but to be persuaded. It is
direct; for it goes to the seat of man's thoughts
and actions. It is more lasting, for what is done
upon a man in the way of outward act, controlling
his conduct, will be much less permanent than
that which is done in his character, sinking down
into his will and wish and purpose, where it is likely
to abide. As we come to measure the methods of
men and to arrange the ways of our own working
in the world, we find, as we see when we look upon
the course of God's providence, that the great
forces are those which work quietly and spiritually,
and not the physical and material forces. Thus it
is with us personally. The men who influence us
most are not those who try to drive us to do their
will. We always resist, by virtue of all that
makes us men, when any one tries to compel us.
One can do almost what he will with us, except
force us into a way in which we do not wish to
walk. By his spirit, by his reasoning, by his persuasion, by the force of his example, by the sweet
benignity of his character and presence, he can
win us to himself. So, when we go out to work
upon others, we come back disappointed and vexed
if we have tried to force a man; but we often
have success when we try to win him. The old

fable is true philosophy; it is not the wind, it is the sun which brings the traveller to its own terms.

In the family, in the school, and even in the care of the criminal and the insane, we find still that with the passing away of that which is violent, and the bringing in of gentler methods, we are caring for children and men in a better way. It is so when we look abroad upon those who go out into the earth and gain power over savages and barbarians. Livingstone drew men to himself by his gentleness and kindness, and he became a father to them. This is the great force of history. The history of our own land is written in a single verse by one of our poets:

> The voice of the Lord by night
> To the watching pilgrims came,
> As they sat by the seaside,
> And filled their hearts with flame.

Whatever may be done by the great movements of armies and nations, the moving force underneath these has been this mighty working of God's spirit through the human will.

Often among men it has been the gentlest, most quiet ministrations which have produced the greatest results. When Edward had starved Calais into surrender, and held the city which he had so long besieged, it was in his power to destroy it; but the people preserved their city and preserved their lives, "not by might." He said that he would spare the city if six of the citizens would give themselves into his hands; and six of the leading men came out, stripped of their raiment, every man with a halter about his neck. They bore the keys of the city; they threw themselves at the king's feet; they gave themselves unreservedly into his hands, and asked for his mercy. They were answered with a call for the executioner. There were his knights, and there was the great army, but they had no power over him. He was the monarch, and all power was with him. Then Philippa knelt at his feet and cried, " Ah, gentle sire, now pray I, and beseech you, with folded hands, for the love of our Lady's son to have mercy upon them ! "

And the king answered, " Lady, I would rather you had been otherwhere. You pray so tenderly that I dare not refuse you; and though I do it against my will, I give them to you." So the lives of the men were spared, the peace of the city was saved, and the honor of the king and the English people was preserved; " Not by might, nor by power," but by the spirit of a woman's prayer.

Or if we look upon the rulers of the world, in the various departments of life, we find the same principle at work. Great armies do not of themselves win the victory. It is the silent counsel of the men at the head of the army. Great statesmen are not by their open deeds controlling men; it is more by the thought wrought out in their chambers. Great artists are not artists by force of physical power, but by a certain spiritual character which belongs to them, which never can be imitated, and into which no training can ever bring a man. An English painter said, "I mix my paint with brains." Guido said of Rubens, "He mixes his paint with blood." Surely it is this genius which, working within a man, makes him able to control others through that which he does before their eyes.

Again the force which works in woman, which gives her that marvellous influence which is scarcely second to anything in the world to-day, is a force which is not gained by noise or by pushing forward into prominence. But in her own place, with her voice, with her example, with her training of children, with all that is beautiful and strong in her character, she gains control of the thought and method of those whose work is more manifest and more resounding through the world. The whole march of civilization is upon this line. Every gain we make is a gain of spiritual over material force. It is the putting away of armies, the forces of war; it is the withholding of physical control; it is bringing out reason, conscience, and those immaterial and invisible forces which have their seat in the heart of man, and have the field of their working in the hearts of other men. As civilization goes on from this immature state towards its completion, more and more shall we find the working not of might, nor power, but of spiritual energy, of spiritual influence over the hearts of men.

If this be so within this little domain of ours, where we have this influence one over another, still more is it true when we reach out into the eternal working of God and seek to find in what way he will bring his own purposes to pass. It is not by great, astounding works — by the thunder of his voice, by the roar of his tempests, by the flashing of his lightning — that God seeks to control men. It is by the Virgin's child, born in a little village, in an obscure province, the spirit of whose life is, "He shall not strive nor cry; neither shall any man hear his voice in the streets;" who is ordained for his ministry by the descent of a dove upon him, and who finds his work in the world when John the Baptist, with his loud voice, has receded; when he baptizes men not with the water of the Jordan, which they could see, and whose flowing, falling drops they could watch, but with the Spirit of the living God in their hearts. Even this is not to be continued. This visible presence must be withdrawn. St. Paul says, "Though I have known Christ after the flesh, yet now henceforth know I him no more." He would not know any one whom he could see; he would not hear any one whose voice fell upon his ear. Only spiritual vision should control him; only spiritual utterances should guide him; for there had come, when the Christ had vanished from the earth, as it was expedient that he should do, the reign of the Spirit, the Holy Spirit, who should, because he is Spirit, control the spirits of men who control themselves and who govern the world.

Hence when we come to this spiritual era we come into an advance, a sudden and marked advance, of this spiritual, unseen agency. That day which stands out from all the days of Pentecost as *the* Day of Pentecost is not thus distinguished by the "sound as of the rushing of a mighty wind," for there had been a rushing, mighty wind ever since there had been a wind to blow. The grand distinguishing peculiarity which separates and signalizes the Day of Pentecost is the coming of a spiritual power, unseen and mysterious, which, descending out of heaven, finds its way into the spirits of men and there works its holy and divine pleasure; and that which is still the highest in all Scripture, as in all human thought, is this spiritual presence.

Brethren, we have come to the beginning of the end. We shall change our place, but shall not advance beyond this period that we are living in. The spiritual reign of God to-day is the beginning of the everlasting reign of God. It is the eternal reign of spirit and of truth in that kingdom which is no longer at Jerusalem; which is not army nor government, palace nor cathedral; which is "righteousness, peace, and joy in the Holy Ghost."

If we pass for a moment to the examination of those things which it is necessary to have done in the world, as our Lord himself has described them — and the catalogue is neither brief nor narrow — we find that every one of them must necessarily be done by the Spirit, if it is done at all. There are certain things which a man can do by outward force. He can fell the tree; he can break the rock; he can shut men in prison; he can drive them by his whip; he can take away their existence in this world, and after that he has no more that he can do. The grand things which must be done must be done by the Spirit of God in the spirit of men. Let us look at the list for a moment.

If a man is to enter upon the life of the sons of God, he must enter upon it in the only way in which life is ever entered upon, and that is by birth. If he is to come into the household of God and be God's child, he must be born into it. There are no orphans in God's house; there are no strangers there. None dwell with God on earth or in heaven except the children of God, and no one becomes God's child except by birth. Hence there comes this need of the new birth. "Ye must be born again," is our first step in righteousness and eternal life. Surely that is a spiritual work. You cannot by any outward demonstration create a man's thoughts over again, renew his purposes, change the current of his life. It must be done within him; and the only thing which can work within him is the Spirit which can enter into a man.

Again, it is necessary that men should be convinced of sin, and of righteousness, and of judgment; and this can only be done by the Spirit of God. It is necessary that some one should take of the things of Christ and show them unto men, and guide men into all truth; and this can only be done by the Spirit. Again, it is necessary that there should be a continual abiding of God with men. Everywhere, in all the homes of men, there must be this divine presence which can only be a spiritual presence. This is to give the witness to us that we are God's children; this is to give us the assurance whereby we can say, "Abba, Father," and look up into the face of Jehovah of hosts. The Spirit comes to us, again, to give us that which is described in the large word of the New Testament, "Comfort." The Comforter must be in the heart of us. You cannot comfort a man when he is in trouble by building him a larger house, or by pouring wealth into his lap. Comfort must find the troubled heart; and the only Comforter of the world is the divine Comforter, who, with all consolation in his hand, bears his solace into the troubled hearts of the children of men.

It is a beautiful suggestion which the Psalmist made long ago. And how many of these old verses of the Psalmists and of the Prophets come out with new light and enlargement when we read them with the New Testament in our hands! The Holy Spirit descended upon our Lord in bodily form as a dove, and he was the Comforter. The emblem of the Holy Spirit in the New Testament is the dove resting upon humanity in the Son of Man. Now read the words of David: " Oh, that I had wings like a dove!" But such wings would not be strong enough to bear us above the trouble and weariness of this world. Read that verse now with the New Testament open before you, and how full of strength it becomes; how full of reality, satisfaction, and power! The devout and longing soul breathes forth a better aspiration: " Oh, that I had the wings of the dove, the Holy Ghost, the Comforter; then would I fly away, borne up on these almighty pinions, into the everlasting rest."

If we take that work which is yet to be done in the world, to win the world unto the love of Christ, still it is the same spiritual work, bringing men into new lives, that they may have a new destiny of righteousness and of eternal life. Truly, as one reads it again, there comes a fresh interpretation of an old Scripture. So many say nowadays that the Old Testament is harsh and unkind. I suppose they say so because they do not read it. You can say what you please about a man whom you do not know. One who knows the Old Testament will not say that. But how beautiful, how enlarged, how strong, how precious, becomes the Old Testament thought in the light of the New. For it was an Old Testament saint who said, "Thy gentleness," thy quietness, thy patience, thy love, not thy might nor thy power, "thy gentleness hath made me great."

Thus it must be always; and we are not surprised at this the moment we think who the Holy Spirit is. It is not the wind, it is not light. It is the spirit of God entering into the spirit of man. The Holy Spirit is God. If any one shall say the Holy Spirit seems sometimes to be spoken of as an influence proceeding into the world, still it is God's influence. There have been persons who have doubted the divinity of Christ; I believe no one doubts the divinity of the Holy Spirit. It is God's influence, if it is an influence. Rather it is God having influence, who is the Holy Spirit. When one thinks how great God is, and how near he can come to us because we are spirit as he is spirit, then he finds the provision for all this that shall come.

Hence we find, passing again from the Old Testament to the New, how a word which there is set aside in the sentence of the Prophet, comes from the lips of the Christ with all its force strengthened, and becomes one of the telling and inspiring words of the Gospel truth. "Not by power," said the Prophet; and Jesus said, "Ye shall receive power after that the Holy Ghost is come upon you." "Not by God's hand," said the Prophet; "By my spirit," said the Christ. "Not by what shall be done outwardly upon men, but by what shall be done in the hearts of men," said the Prophet. " Ye shall receive power over the hearts of men," Jesus taught, when on the Mount of the Ascension he gave his last promise to the disciples whom he was to leave in the world. The power is that which makes human efficiency and accomplishment.

Knowledge is said to be power. Knowledge is power in the same sense that wood is fuel. Wood on fire is fuel; knowledge on fire is power. There is no more power in knowledge than there is in the stones or stars which you know, unless there be a spirit and life in the knowledge which give it its energy. In proportion as men have this spiritual power do they become strong in the world. If I may borrow the illustration from one of our own writers ; when Eric starts from Greenland in robust health he will steer west, and his ships will reach Newfoundland. But take out Eric and put in Biorne or Thorfin, and with just as much ease the ship will find New England. The difference between Eric and Biörnö is a difference of spirit. The difference between Peter on the day of Pentecost and Peter before is a difference of spiritual power. Hear his last question before he comes to the Ascension : " Lord, and what shall this man do ? " Hear his question on the Mount of the Ascension : " Wilt thou at this time restore again the kingdom to Israel?" Hear his words when the Spirit of God has descended upon him; words which have never ceased; which have brought men by the thousands into the new life by the cross. Take Saul of Tarsus with all his madness; he learns no new philosophy at Damascus, gains nothing of that which is accounted knowledge. There comes upon him, after he has gone into the city, the Holy Ghost, and St. Paul from that hour outstrips all others in the greatness of his accomplishment in the hearts and lives of men.

Power comes to knowledge to give it efficiency. Knowledge without power is like the heir-apparent to the throne. He is of royal blood, but he has no authority. Knowledge with power is the prince on the throne, with the crown and sceptre. Power comes to good resolution to give it efficiency. This is weak; it is worthless in itself. "I will arise and go to my father," is a purpose, and the man is as hungry and as ragged after it as he was before. "I arise and go to my father;" that is resolution with power in it. Duty comes to us as something hard, and we shrink from it. No one is a large man if he does not feel that his duty is larger than himself. Our ideas of duty are too petty, and too low, if we are able of ourselves to change them into the deeds. It never was meant that a man by himself should do his work. The Sermon on the Mount is beyond every one of us. But with the Sermon on the Mount comes the promise of power by which we can meet its duties; and when we take the commandment with the power which accompanies it, then we can do our duty. God who gives the duty gives himself to make us strong for the duty. "When religion ceases to demand the impossible, it ceases to be religion," some one has said, and it is a simple and profound truth. So in our way of attainment. We look at these visions of Christian character, and how far beyond us they seem as they are presented in the New Testament? And who can ever come up to this excellency of heart and of life, to be perfect, to be holy? We do well to despair and say, "It is a dream, this thought of being so great. It may be for apostles; it may be for pious women; it is not for business men." It is for business men. Business men are to be saints. Business is to be as holy as praying, or we have no right to touch it with one of our fingers; and our common occupations are to be as holy as the work of the angels. Can it ever be? Of course it can never be. Let us abandon all hope of it. Then let us make it true. For Jesus says, when he sets before us this lofty ideal, I will give you power; I will bear your thoughts up; I will inspire your purposes; I will attend you through all the strain and stress of life, and you shall be clean, for I will make you pure. When Christ keeps a man, there is not pollution enough in the world to stain his garments; there is not heat enough in the furnace to put the smell of fire even upon his robes.

Or, if we think of Christian work which we are to do for men as ministers of God's grace, again we shrink from it. How can we bring men to the Saviour? "It is of no use for me to speak to my neighbor," a man says. "There is very little comes from preaching the gospel," men say. "There is very little good comes from the Sabbath-school," some think. There is truth in these words and thoughts. Not by the might of words, not by the power of preaching, when a man's lips utter the truth to human ears, can the work be done. But when the school becomes filled with the Spirit of God; when in every teacher's heart is the Holy Spirit speaking through his lips; when the Spirit of God gives you truth to utter, and prepares the heart of the one to whom you shall speak it, and when you obey the Spirit, then your ministry becomes a power in the world.

It is not strange that our lives seem to us so weak. There are some of you who are wont to express your discontent with life and its results. You are discontented and it will grow worse and worse. You will go through a series of disappointments, and on your dying bed you will say that life is a failure, and it may be you will tell the truth. It may be a failure. It is a pity to work hard fifty years and then die with little done. But we do. We are not equal to life; we cannot bear its temptations; we cannot meet its duties; we cannot fulfil our purposes; and it is in vain that we rely upon might and power. "But have I not all my years attended church?" one may ask. "Do I not try very hard to do right?" Very likely. "Not by might" do men do right; "not by power" do men fulfil the end of their being, "but by my spirit, saith the Lord of hosts." Only God is as great as a human life. A man is not large enough for that which God requires of him, since sin has shrunken him to small proportions. If you will let the Spirit of God come into your heart and make your thoughts; if you will let him mark out your path day by day, and then tread it; if you will listen to his suggestions and obey his word, to-day will be successful, to-morrow will be prosperous. Men will praise you, and, better than that, your heart will commend you. Then, and never until then, will the voice of the Christ say "Well done, good and faithful servant."

I would save you, and I would save myself, from narrow and earthly living. I would come with you into these high and holy purposes which shall accomplish great results. But it is not by external means; it is not by the struggle of our spirits; it is not by the force of our will; it is only as the great, wise, and loving will of the Spirit of God enters into our spirit, that we become great enough. I read only last week the instruction of an actor touching those things which are requisite for success in his calling. This writer said that there are three things necessary: talent, training — but these two would not accomplish much; there must also be what was called "inspiration." I said, "Saul also is among the prophets." If to personate somebody else; if to go through an hour's mimicry for the entertainment of a throng; if to amuse without much prospect of improving; if this demands more than talent and more than training, even a spirit within, then to be real men and to do a real work which shall make the streets safer, which shall make life happier, which shall bring the kingdom of God nearer, this demands more than might — the might of human strength; more than power — the power of a trained will. It demands "My spirit, saith the Lord of hosts." I suppose that we get as much return from life as we have any right to expect. Our might can only repeat the poverty of the recompense, till our failing breath shall say, "Vanity of vanities." Where is our wisdom to-day, but in opening our hearts to the strength which never fails; to the incoming of the life which is the beginning of immortality! Then shall we reign; then shall we do our daily work in the power and glory of it. Then shall man be served, and God be glorified.

It is this — let me say again — it is this which the world needs. They tell us the Church has lost its power in the world. It is not true. But the

Church will enlarge its influence when it has enlarged its spirit. The greatest gift which you can give to your profession, to your house, to the community, is the gift of a man who lives by the power of God's Spirit teaching him, directing him, employing him, and who shall carry down into all the sordidness and earthiness of the world a spiritual character, spiritual utterances, spiritual vision; a life that is made up by the power of the endless years.

I turn from this subject with regret. As I stand with you to-day and see how life promises to repeat its inefficiency, and that many of us are likely to lie down at last defeated, and perhaps in the grave of the wicked, I cannot cease from saying to you and to myself, that there is but one thing which can save us; but one way in which we can glorify God in our heart and our life; and that is, not by simply trying to be good; not by working hard to do good; it is by receiving the Spirit into our spirit; praying God to come to us and take us; to teach us, to guide us, to use us. Then God's success shall be our success; life shall be glorified, and God shall be honored.

There stands the organ, as it has stood through these minutes in which I have been speaking to you. Unless it falls in pieces, it may stand there for many years, silent as at this moment. There is no voice in its pipes; no sound issues from it. It is dumb; it is dead. If the skilled hands of the player touch the keys, you will hear the rattle, but there will be no music. Handel himself might come and lay his fingers, heavy with melody, upon the keys; there would be the same rattle which a boy could make. Dumb organ, dead, let the sexton bury it out of our sight. There is only one thing which can save it: a breath from without; a spirit which shall come as the wind comes. The air which is in this great outer world must be breathed into its pipes, and answer to the hands of a man, pouring out its obedient harmony. It will wake to music, and to thought, and life, and worship, only as the breath of the living God moves through its silence. If it be true of an organ, it is true of a man. Only as God breathes through our reason and conscience; breathes through these lips and out of this life of ours, only then shall we utter the melody which will enlarge the harmony of the world and blend with the eternal minstrelsy of the supernal courts.

Come, Holy Spirit, heavenly dove,
With all thy quickening powers.

Brethren, it is your last hope. But it is a hope.

VIII.

GRIEVING THE HOLY SPIRIT.

SCRIPTURE LESSON: *Romans* viii: 14-30.
TEXT: Grieve not the Holy Spirit of God. *Eph.* iv: 30.

THIS brings the Holy Spirit very near to us. We must be in intimate relations with him, if we can grieve him. He is no longer afar off; he is not indifferent to our words or our will; he is close to us, tenderly regarding us, intimately interested in us, if what we can do can grieve the Spirit of God, who is the spirit of blessedness.

We are reminded again by this teaching of the personality of the Spirit. You cannot grieve a thing; you cannot grieve an influence; nothing can be grieved but that which has a heart, and a will, and a life — a person. The Holy Spirit is the Spirit of God; God is spirit; God is the Holy Spirit; the Holy Spirit is God.

It is clear that it is a matter of extreme concern that, if God be so near to us, we who would receive his blessing should be submissive to his will; should be governed by his guidance; should let him pour upon us the riches of his grace. It must be a sad thing if one, for any reason, shuts himself out from the blessing and grace of God; if he grieves God so that he withdraws his presence and the man fails of those things which the lavish mercy would bestow upon him — the exceeding richness of his grace.

The Spirit coming into the world to bless us does not come on an independent mission. Let us notice, first of all, the precise position of the work of the Spirit of God. "God so loved the world, that he gave his only-begotten Son, that whosoever believeth in him should not perish, but have everlasting life." The Son of God so loved the world that he gave himself, that men might have everlasting life. The Father and the Son so loved the world that they gave the Holy Spirit that men might have everlasting life. Between the love which is in the heart of God and that love possessing the heart of a man, ruling it and blessing it, stands the cross of Christ who is the incarnate and crucified love of God. The work of the Holy Spirit is to bring this love which is in God's heart, and which works so wondrously and graciously in the cross of the Son of God, into our lives, to make it effective there, that the highest purpose of God may be accomplished; that the greatest thought of the love of God may fulfil itself within the lives of men. This is the work of the Spirit of God which we are to recognize and to think upon. He comes to us to do nothing of himself. Most expressive is that word of the blessed Lord: "The Holy Spirit shall not speak of himself." Precisely as Jesus asserted his oneness with the Father when he said, I am so united with the Father that it is not possible I should do anything as separate from him; I can only do that which I do in union with him; so does he say of the spirit, apart from the Father and apart from me, he can do nothing. It is by the Spirit of God, taking the love of God and the redemption of Christ and carrying them into the spirit of men, that the first and the last thought of God is accomplished in the hearts of his children.

We have but to turn to those things which Christ said concerning the Spirit if we would find the special work which he is to do. We may divide it, in a general way, into three parts. There are three things, or three classes of things, which our Lord has told us that the Holy Spirit will do. In the first place, "He shall glorify me;" that is, he shall show me to the world; he shall make my glory to shine before men. What a testimony it is to our Lord Jesus Christ, that God comes into the world to glorify him! Of what man could it be said, of what angel could it be said, that the great work of God in the world is to glorify him? Yet our Lord said, that the work of the Holy Ghost in the world is to make Christ glorious. "He shall glorify me." "He shall testify of me; he shall take of mine and shall show it unto you;" that is, he shall stand in the stead of Christ that men may see Christ.

Secondly. "He shall guide you into all truth;" not through all truth, but into all truth; not into all departments of truth, the scientific, and philosophical, and historical, but into, within, all that truth which is concerned in the love and in the redemption of God. "He shall show you things to come."

Thirdly. He shall work within the spirit of a man, that the will of God may be done there. Since the evil in man is his departure from God, the Holy Spirit shall bring him back to God. Since man is fallen from his divine nature, the Spirit shall restore him to the divine nature, that he may begin again in life; that, with the old become new, he may make up a new life. To this end he shall make men feel their need of Christ, by reproving them of sin. He shall make them feel the power of Christ, by showing them his redemption which is crowned by his resurrection. He shall make them feel the eternal separation between right and wrong, which is called the judgment, by revealing to them the essential difference and the everlasting difference between one who serves God and one who does not serve God.

Thus, if we take these three departments of life — the glorifying Christ, the guiding into the truth, and the making the truth practically effective within the minds of men — we get, in a general way, the work which the Holy Spirit is to do in the world. He is to bring men to Christ personally, and unite them to him, and then he is to guide them along the Christian life. Hence you find that he is spoken of under various terms, all implying this enlightenment and this elevation of the life. He is the "Holy Spirit." He is the "spirit of grace." He is the "spirit of glory." He is the "spirit of promise." He is the "spirit of God." He is the "spirit of Christ." He is the Holy Spirit — holy in himself, being the very nature of God, and so doing a holy work in the hearts of the children of men. As many as are led by him, they are the sons of God; and as many as have the witness of the Spirit in their spirit that they are born of God, are able, out of the heart, to repeat the words which any one can say with his lips, "Abba Father."

If it be asked in what way this Spirit in our hearts does this work, how this will of God is accomplished by the Spirit, it is evident, at the outset, that we must say he does it by a spiritual presence and a spiritual power. The work is not something which can be described in the terms of our ordinary language, because our ordinary terms are separate from it. It comes by the influence of the Spirit which we are like and of which we are born, upon our spirits which are born of him. Sometimes men may be called by an outward demonstration of might or of power; but the work of the Spirit is the work of God upon the hearts of men. Hence you are not to look for anything surprising in the external world. There will be no new star in the heavens; there may be no great commotion in society; there may be no revolution in your own house. If God does anything for you, he will do it quietly and gently and simply in the heart of you, giving it a new thought, or a stronger thought, a new impulse, a new impression; a changed direction; something of which the world will know nothing at the time; of which you may know little, perhaps, unless you are sensitive to the touch of a friend, sensitive to the influence of a spirit upon your spirit. The prophet is roused by the wind and by the fire; but God is not in the wind nor the fire. These are to awaken him; then God speaks to his attentive ear, and the man wraps his face in his mantle and stands at the entering in of the cave and hears the command and comfort of God. God often rouses us by these outward demonstrations of his power, that we may listen to the quiet speaking of his voice.

The work of the Holy Spirit in us will employ various methods. In the first place, it will be a direct spiritual influence upon our hearts; the Spirit of God coming into contact with our spirit, touching it, affecting it, as light flows into light, as air flows into air, as water flows into water, simply passing through our spirit, as light passes through a crystal, which is one of the illustrations that have been given. Again, the Spirit will oftentimes come to us through our conscience, quickening it, making it speak with a more authoritative voice. He will come again through our reason, guiding us by our processes of thought to certain conclusions which are in accordance with the will of God. Again, he will come to us through our experience, teaching us the lessons of our own life and impressing them upon us until we are wiser by that through which we have passed. Again, he will come to us through the opportunities of life, which is one of his favorite ways of approach, showing us what we may do, and what we ought to do, only that he may reveal to us the will of God, and may bring us up into that which is higher and holier in life. Again, and more especially, he will come to us through the truth of God. If holy men as they were moved by God have written the Scriptures, men are to read the Holy Scriptures as they are moved by him. He will take the word out of the lips of prophet and apostle; he will take the word of Christ, which to-day to us may have no meaning; and he will repeat the word, and make us think upon it, and feel it, until the word becomes light and life to our soul. He will speak to us through the truth uttered by the preacher's voice, by the teacher's, by the father's or mother's, oftentimes by words which have gained power because the lips which uttered them have turned to dust. How many of the memories of life, repeating the truths which those have spoken who have fallen upon sleep, are simply the way which the Holy Spirit takes, uttering his truth in language from which we cannot turn away, in a voice whose tones have become sweeter to us because we have lost sight of the face which was before us when they were spoken; taking the words of a sainted father or of a holy mother, and in their language, in the very tones of their voice, trying to repeat to us the thought of God. You say it is your father speaking to you; it is the Holy Ghost speaking through a father's voice. You say you have tender memories of your mother; the Holy Spirit comes through those recollections, thinking that now he has the word which you cannot resist, that at least you will hear her who was the dearest to you, and that he may persuade you into the ways of God. He will come again through the Church and its ordinances and its sacraments, which have no grace by virtue of their nature, but which are made the vehicle of the grace of God to men.

It is evident that in all these ways it is the purpose of God to find our hearts, and it is the method of God to enter into our hearts, that there he may control us. The Spirit of God does not come to add a cubit to our stature. He does not make one hair white or black. He may not enlarge our resources. He may not strengthen our intellect — yet I suppose he does. If I am not mistaken, a man has a stronger mind and stronger reasoning faculties, he has a larger intellect, when God is in his mind. A man's power to study and grasp truth, all the truth of God, in nature, in religion, in science and in philosophy, is greatest when the man's mind and heart are full of the Spirit of the living God.

But it will be asked, how, if these things are to be discerned spiritually, and are to be the spiritual working of God in us, can we bring him to us that this power shall become a reality in our experience? If it were a man, we might call him; if it were a school, we might enter it; if it were a book, we might read it. But if it be the coming of spirit into spirit, what can we who are in the flesh do, that he may enter into us? The question indicates a common mistake. Strange that men should think that there is something we must do in order to bring God near to us, when God is as close to us as our own life; when within God we are living and moving. They cannot have read the Bible if they think that in some way they must search the heavens to bring God down, or descend into the depths to bring God up. He is near our hearts to-day. What is the whole representation of Scripture? That God is speaking to us, and is so near that we can hear his voice. What is the promise to prayer? That God's ear is so near that he hears us, even when we do not lisp the words. How shall God be nearer to a man than that? Is he not always calling us, not waiting to be called of us? Is he not always pleading with us, entreating us, warning us, that he may bring us to himself? How vivid is that language of Scripture: "Behold, I stand at the door and knock." Let me warn you against the error, that, staying within your bolted doors, you must wait for God to come down out of the heavens; lifting up your voice, beseeching him to come, that you may feel his presence. If you would stop talking long enough, you would hear his knock at the door; if you would be still long enough, you would find his finger at the latch; if you would only open your heart, you would find him within the heart.

Yet are we not told in the Scriptures that we must ask for the Holy Spirit? Is it not said that God will give the Holy Spirit to them that ask him? Yes; but in what connection is it said? It is said that God will give the Holy Spirit as a loving father will give bread to his children — bread, the staff of life; the spirit, the staff of life. But how does the father give to his child? Are your children in the habit of begging you for bread? Do they go to bed at night anxious lest there should be no food for them? Do you not provide the bread, and place it upon the table, and summon them to eat, perhaps oftentimes compel them to go in? The asking of a child for bread is answered before it is heard. Your child has not prayed for his daily bread for this noon and this evening, but you have it ready. He may ask, but there is no need of begging. The prayer for the Holy Spirit will be the natural expression of desire. We should ask out of a heart which knows that it will have the blessing as it is sure of the Father's love and has the Father's promise, and his presence. We must open the heart, open the nature, open the spirit, and let the Spirit come in.

The light as it shines out of the heavens falls upon the marble, plays upon its surface, brightens it for a moment, but does not pass within it. The marble is not open to the light. The same light falls upon the diamond, harder than marble, passes into it, and there divides its own brightness, its purple and its gold, and flashes it out before the eyes of men. Be not the marble, and let the Spirit of God lie upon the stony heart. Be the diamond, and let the Spirit of God enter into the heart to enlighten it, to linger in it, to make it bright and beautiful, until men shall behold its glory as it is illumined with the glory of God. But for this it is necessary to put far from us all alien things — the unholy thing, that we may have holiness; the selfish thing, that we may have charity; the earthly thing, that we may have the heavenly. We must give all we have; part with all our pearls for a better one, sell all our land for a field with a treasure in it; give up ourselves to find God; give up this world to find heaven; give up our sin to find righteousness; give up to-day to find the endless years.

We are to obey Christ if we would have the Holy Spirit. He said, "If ye love me, keep my commandments, and I will pray the Father, and he shall give you another Comforter, that he may abide with you forever." Do the will of the Christ, and you shall have the Spirit of the Christ.

Perhaps it will be said that these methods which I have sketched are rather the result; that they are the things to be obtained through the Spirit, rather than the method by which we may receive the Spirit. I think the point is well taken; yet one falls naturally into this way of speaking. Before you open your heart to the Spirit, the Spirit must enter your heart himself, that is true. Before you obey Christ, the Spirit of Christ must come to you.

Suppose, then, we change the thought for a moment. What am I to do that I may receive the Holy Spirit? A man can have the Spirit of God by consenting to his influence. Yield to him and he will stay with you; consent to his control and he will control you; be willing to be holy and he will make you holy. This whole matter of bringing the Holy Spirit into the control of our life and into the sanctifying of our body and of our spirit may be set in a single word; and that word is *obedience*. He who will obey God's Spirit shall have God's Spirit; shall be guided by him, and that forevermore. There is no royal road but this. If you want the Spirit of God to control you, he will.

I think that there is nothing told us in the New Testament of the method in which we are to bring the Holy Spirit to us. God seems to have taken that entirely into his own hands. You will find these promises repeated: "The Father will send the Spirit," "The Spirit will come to you." We are dependent. Let God choose the method of his own work. He promises that the spirit shall abide with us, if we want him; not as a stranger or a guest, or a servant, but as a friend. We are to want him, and be sensitive to his presence, and we shall have the Spirit of God.

We can make this a little more distinct, perhaps, by recalling the things which the Holy Spirit is to do. He has three departments of work: first, he is to glorify Christ. The Spirit of God when he comes to you will seek to glorify Christ. If he points to Christ, you are to look to Christ. If he repeats the words of Christ, you are to hear them. If he lays down the commands of Christ, you are to receive them. He seeks to make Christ great and glorious in your eyes; and if you will let Christ be glorified, then the Holy Spirit will intensify the glory forever. Secondly, he is to guide into all truth. If you want to be guided into all truth, then enter into all truth. Take the Word of God; open it before you; let the Spirit of God interpret it; and when you have found a truth, believe it; when you have found a promise, trust it; when you have found a command, do it. Yield to this touch which comes up through the words of Scripture, and the Holy Spirit will bless the truth to you. If he tells you that this is the path to walk in, walk in it, and he will lead you to the end. Then thirdly, if he is to regenerate us, if he is to bring us out of unrighteousness into holiness, let us consent to take up the new plans of life; to take out of our life everything that is unholy; to consent to do right and to be wholly right with God; to consent to have our spirit sanctified and to have the earnest of that sanctifying which is to make even this vile body a spiritual body like our Lord's.

It was a very striking remark, an interesting thought, of one of my predecessors in this ministry. He made a voyage around the world a few years ago, and in his leisure he wrote a sermon. He tells us how much he was impressed by one thing on shipboard; and that was the man at the wheel. Summer and winter, all through the voyage, there stood that man. The captain might be away; the crew might be absent; everybody else but this one man and the officer of the deck might be asleep, might be at worship, might be engaged in any of the affairs of the ship, but there, through day and night, was that constant man at the wheel. The touch of his hand governed the ship, ordered the sails, guarded the treasure of merchandise and men. The ship was in the control, under the captain, of that man's will, of his virtue, of his power,—of that man's spirit. Now the remark to which I alluded was this: Doctor Adams says, "The suggestions of the Holy Spirit are the man at the wheel in our souls." I will leave you to think it out.

I have not forgotten the words which I read as the text. This which I have said is an illustration, an unfolding of that word of the apostle, "Grieve not the Holy Spirit of God." If any one shall ask how may I grieve the Holy Spirit, I can only say by failing to do this which I have described. Neglecting him, that is grieving him. Refuse to listen, that is grieving him; refuse to obey, that is grieving him. Make him know that you do not want him, and after a time he will go his way and you will be left to yourself. There is but one way to possess him permanently, and that is to obey him. There is but one way to grieve him, and that is to neglect him. The ship answers to her helm, and the will of the man is done. The life answers to the Spirit, and the will of the Spirit is done. We think his thoughts, we are governed by his purposes, and thus we honor him and have his power. We leave him, and he leaves us. There are other words beside these. St. Paul was fond of the tender words. There are different words which describe the same thing. Thus, Isaiah speaks of "wearying" God. Do you suppose you could stand and knock at a man's door as long as God has knocked at yours, and not be tired of it? Ezekiel uses another word; he speaks of "fretting" God. It is a strange word. You know what it means; to be annoyed and hindered; not to be struck or denounced, only to be worried. We may do this by thinking of the Spirit and then forgetting him; going a little way with him, and then turning back; professing great things on Sunday, and on Monday denying them. It is an admirable word. It would fret you to have your child do so; and Ezekiel says that God is fretted, speaking after the manner of men. Then the author of the Epistle to the Hebrews says, that we may "do despite," malice, wrong, cruelty, unto the Spirit of God. Perhaps the strongest use of the word which here is translated "grieve," is in the account of our Lord's suffering in Gethsemane, where it is said that he became "exceeding sorrowful." The word for "sorrowful" is this word "grieve." I do not like to say it, but it seems like making a Gethsemane in our hearts, to resist the Holy Spirit. Jesus entered into the garden and began to be "exceeding sorrowful." Do not make the Holy Spirit "exceeding sorrowful." God is trying all the time to help you, all the while to teach you and to save you, to exalt you, and if you are persistently slighting, wounding, bruising him, until the soul becomes the garden with the olive-trees, then is the Saviour, the Comforter of men, "exceeding sorrowful." Grieve not the Holy Spirit of God.

There is another spirit; it is the spirit of the world. It is a spirit in men and women; St. Paul called it " the course of this world," and " the prince of the power of the air." It works against the Spirit of God, and it strives to draw us away from Christ and the things of Christ; and often it succeeds. I have seen this spirit of the world come to men. The Spirit of God had been trying to win them to Christ the Saviour. They were almost persuaded, until there came this other spirit, touching their thoughts and turning them the other way; touching the affections and turning them from God. It comes like an angel of light, of course; it has wings which shine in the partial light, and it wins men from God; they turn away from Christ; they think less upon him; they give up their good purposes; they become more and more earthy, until their spiritual nature hardens and shrinks. The spirit of the world binds men hand and foot. Still the Spirit of God will break the bands if men will let him; but the bands are tight and strong, and many a man is dragged to his death by the unholy spirit, the spirit of this world, the prince of the power of the air.

I wish that were the whole; but sometimes this spirit of the world comes even into a heart into which the Spirit of God has entered. A man makes his confession of Christ and enters the Church. He becomes zealous for the good of others. He runs well for a time, as St. Paul said, and you picture for him a noble career, until presently he becomes inconstant; drops a service here and there; has less and less interest in divine things. He says his business requires it, which is not true. He says the necessities of this world require it, though they never do. The spirit of the world tells him, "You cannot afford to be an earnest Christian man. Give that over to people of leisure. You, with your peculiar temperament, were never made to be useful; with your circumstances it was never expected that you would be a witness for Christ. You, with the society you move in, with your associates, with your pleasures—how hopeless it is for you to try to be a Christian." It is said that it is hard to be a Christian in these days. If it is, it is not because the Spirit of God is not here, but because the spirit of this world is here; and many a Christian heart gives up its faith, casts away its joy and its strength, sinks into uselessness, and makes itself more and more the centre of itself, until the Spirit of God is grieved. I will not say how far a man may go in doing despite to the Spirit of God and yet attain to heaven at last.

But it is so sad that a man should go to heaven alone, and that all the path which he treads should be filled with a grieving of the Holy Spirit.

What is the remedy? Why, simply yielding to the Holy Spirit. If he inspires you with any new thought, take it; if he tells you there is something to be done, do it; if it is impressed upon you that there is something to say, say it; if he comes with prohibition, let the prohibited thing alone. Expect nothing but the gentle touch upon your heart. If anything interferes with your spiritual welfare, leave it. The Holy Spirit means to use your work and your play; to use your learning and your life. You are not to cut off the right hand unless it offends; you are not to spare it if it does offend you.

This subject is one of extreme solemnity. But I have to leave you, as it is always best for a preacher to do, unto the divine guidance; and I do it with this word. If there is borne in upon your thought and mind to-day the feeling of anything which you ought to do, obey the impulse. Trust God and move on. The first step in the spiritual life is the first step towards the eternal glory. It is not difficult to understand that sin against the Holy Ghost which hath no forgiveness. It is the final parting of the soul from God. When God the Father comes, if he is rejected, there remain the Son and the Spirit. When God the Son comes, if he is rejected, there remains still the Spirit. Christ may bring a man to the Father, the Spirit may bring a man to the Son, and so to the Father; but when one has despised the Holy Spirit, there is nothing beyond.

If I may use such an expression, a man has three chances in life. He can make up his life under God the Father, If he 'loses that, he may perhaps make it up under the Son. If he loses that he may perhaps make it up under the Spirit. But if he loses the Spirit of God, there is nothing afterwards; no covenant mercy, no encouragement. A man has nothing to hope for, if the love of God has not held him, and the cross of Christ has not won him, and the Spirit of God cannot persuade him.

The unpardonable sin against the light is to put out the eyes. The unpardonable sin against food is to refuse to eat. The unpardonable sin against God is not to let God govern us and save us. The unpardonable sin is to throw away the last of a man's three chances of life; to refuse that Spirit which, moving in our spirits, would bring us to Christ the Saviour, and to God the Father of us all.

> O Spirit, beautiful and dread!
> My heart is fit to break
> With love of all thy tenderness
> For us poor sinners' sake.

IX.

TURNING NORTHWARD.

[A NEW YEAR'S SERMON.]

SCRIPTURE LESSON : *Phil.* Chapter iii.
TEXT: Ye have compassed this mountain long enough; turn you northward. *Deut.* ii: 3.

THIS was Mount Seir. The children of Israel had come thus far on their way towards the land which they were to possess. They tarried around the mountain. It was not Egypt, with its bondage, its idolatry, and its despair; but it was not the land of promise, with its wealth, its opportunity, and its blessings. It was not here in the wilderness that they were to build the city of God, to raise up the prophets and apostles of the world, and to form a State and Church which would represent the kingdom of God upon the earth. Yet they lingered; they compassed the mountain many days, until at last the word of him who had called them out of Egypt found them: "Ye have compassed this mountain long enough; turn you northward."

It comes to us very often in life to need the summons which came to these our brethren. We are inclined to remain where we are. We become engrossed with certain pursuits and pleasures, and come to think that life has found its limits and henceforth must be little but repetition; until the voice of God comes to us, sometimes speaking in our conscience, sometimes through a world which calls us to higher duty, sometimes directly by the Spirit of God in our spirit, sometimes through the providence which tears us away from our place, or removes those things which have detained us. Thus are we made to take up again the way and the work of life that we may finish that whereunto we are created. There are two movements in this world. They have been aptly described as the circular and the onward movement. The one is that movement by which a man goes the round of his daily duties from week to week. and from year to year, repeating over and over those things which it is well for him to do, yet making no advance. There is another movement wherein a man, fulfilling the course of his ordinary duties, still makes an advance, going farther and farther from the place where he started and towards that which is to be the crown and reward and rest of his life. A very obvious illustration is in the motion of the earth, with its circular movement upon its axis, yet with that which is its larger movement by which it pushes on continually, day by day, in a larger orbit around the point which is the centre of its life. Or, if this be too contracted an illustration, this whole system to which we belong preserves its circular movement; it compasses the mountain, yet all the while, through centuries which are unnumbered, it is pressing on its way around some remote sun which no man's eyes have ever yet beheld, in an orbit which only the cycles of the ages can complete. Our life is to be after this double pattern. We are to repeat those things which each day demands; yet, as we do them, we are to press our way around some distant centre in an endless course. There are certain things which must be done day after day, as long as we live. The necessities of life are continually recurring and with very little change; and there comes to us a great economy of time because we acquire great facility in execution, through this continual repetition, until they demand very little thought, and to do them becomes almost a second nature, or the instinctive work of life. The great danger is not that we shall neglect these things, though possibly we need a word of admonition at that point, and to be reminded that we are not to despise the things which are small, the common daily duties, those things without which life would be out of joint, and nothing great could be accomplished. The very monotony of life marks the stability of purpose and method which we have learned of God. But the greater danger is, that we shall mistake this continual movement for an advance, and shall think that we are doing all which really is required of us, and all that we can do for ourselves, if we are continually busy. If all the while we are doing something, and that something is a useful thing, we may assume that we are fulfilling the great end of life. So we shall settle down into that which is simple and monotonous, and never advance, however much the years may come within our reach; reading as we have read, feeling as we have felt, going through life with the same design, and filling up the life that comes to us out of the same methods with the life that has passed from us.

I think we hear to-day, as the year closes, the voice of God speaking to us, not as the children of Israel, not as any special men and women in any special time, but speaking that which men all the ages through have needed to hear; the summons of God to something more, bidding us press on to that which is still beyond us, if so be we may make life greater than it is. It is unquestionably true that we have trodden the rounds of another twelvemonth, every one of us. It is certainly true that we have slept and waked, we have been eating and drinking, we have gone forth to our work in the morning, and we have come home at night, we have filled up the months, and we think we have been very much engaged. It is a doubtful matter, at the best, whether we have simply been treading round and round in the same little circle, or whether we have succeeded in taking one step beyond our past. This is the last day of the year — of what year? This year of grace which we call 1882. Is it also the last day of 1881, 1880, 1879, 1859? Is it the same old ending of a year which finds us still tracing the same circle? If we are not wiser than we were a year ago, if we are not stronger for God and ourselves, this is not the close of 1882 much more than it is the close of 1881, or 1880; and so far as advance and profit is concerned, we might almost as well have slept through the months, to have been aroused by the new-year's bell, which tells that the train is pushing on from another station along the same dull track. It is such a different thing to exist and to breathe, and to reckon the days by the calendar, and to "grow old," as we say, from what it is to grow better and stronger, to make the world feel your presence, and to win the favor of Heaven, that it comes as a word of benediction while it is a word of summons to our spirits: "Ye have compassed this mountain long enough; you have done these things long enough; you have had these methods, and hopes, and desires long enough; you are too old to keep them; life is too great for you to maintain them; turn you northward into something better than you have done, and into something greater than you are."

If I may indicate one or two points in which this advance may be made, merely touching them, it is that we may see how it is possible to enlarge our life. First, in the way of knowledge. We ought, in this coming year — for it is of the year to come, and not of the year that has gone, that I speak — to enlarge our knowledge. We shall be reading: we ought to read better books, a higher grade of books; as our children will pass on to books which are more advanced, so ought we who are older. There are books which will task the energies of any one of us. We ought to grow wiser by that which we read. If it is simply reading the paper which is no more to-day than it was yesterday; if it is reading the current gossip which does not change in character from year to year; if it is not taking hold of something which will enlarge the substance of our knowledge, then we shall read to very little purpose. We enlarge our knowledge, too, by talking with men. We ought to associate with better men, if we can, than those who have surrounded us. We certainly can associate with the wisest men, and when they are at their best, if we will take their books, if we will take the influence of their lives as it comes to us through their works. Out of this will come in that which shall strengthen our own knowledge, enlarge our own minds. To think how many good men are waiting for us if we will break from frivolous companions; to think how many grand books are waiting patiently for us that we may take them up and take their wisdom into us; this should make us feel that there is something to be learned, and something which we ought to learn.

But passing from knowledge to work, we can enlarge our work. Very likely we can enlarge our common work; enlarge the volume of it. It is almost certain that we can enlarge the character of it, taking on some things which are higher, and in advance of those which we have done. We can enlarge our charitable work as it reaches out to bless the world, if we have gained that secret of all true living, that we are in the world and taught of God that we may bless the world; and that the gains of life come to us not to be kept, but to be shared with others.

Again, take the matter of character. We can keep the character we have to-day, which is reasonably honest, and amiable, and pleasant, which does not very much reproach us, or draw to us the reproach of others; or we can strengthen that character. We can enlarge our conscience, we can broaden our reason, we can get a stronger and fuller grasp upon truth, we can get a higher and holier sense of duty, we can get hold of the very meaning of life, we can ask and answer the profound inquiries, "Why am I here? Why has God in his mercy kept me out of my grave for another year? Why do I look with bold eyes down these opening months?" We can enlarge the purposes of life, the motives which shall control life. We can enlarge the desire of life ; that which shall give its support and its character to the very soul and heart which lies behind that which we are doing before men. Thus our manhood shall grow by the continual accession of truth, and the continual performance of duty.

Finally, we can enlarge our religion, on the side of its worship and on the side of its work. It is not enough to tread the round of Sabbaths and to come and go through the gates of the sanctuary; it is not enough to have stated hours of prayer and holy communion, and to be content with these. We can enlarge religious experience until it is deeper and broader. We can enlarge religious work until it tells more for good upon the world. Prayer should be to us what it has never been, and the Bible more than it ever has been; these varied means of grace, which are the summons to duty, should give to us that largeness of spirit and that greatness of religious accomplishment which shall make us more like the Son of God and the Saviour of men. We ought to outgrow that weakness which makes our religion chiefly regard ourselves. That momentous question which is asked so often, and for which sometimes we claim merit, was the question of a frightened Pagan. We ought to have outgrown it. There is no one of us who should not have left it behind him years ago: " What must I do to be saved ? " Have we not answered that, and taken the answer practically into our lives? That question should be changed into the affirmation of the Son of God, which reaches beyond the question which looks to our own salvation, and teaches the divine motive of all worthy living, "Father, I have glorified thee upon the earth: I have finished the work which thou gavest me to do."

It is evident that in these four respects which I have named, we can gain accessions of that which is valuable to us without making any advance. Thus, we can enlarge our knowledge without enlarging our manhood. We may be just as selfish after we have doubled our learning as we were before; and unless we grow less selfish, we do not grow more manly. Manhood is not high learning; the tree of knowledge never has been, and never can be, the tree of life. He who thinks he is fulfilling his life by increasing his knowledge, has made the fearful mistake of supposing that the value of things is in their bulk. The value of things is in their character, not their size. So, passing from knowledge into work, we still may enlarge our work without growing any greater or making any advance. That work may still keep its old centre, the self. I may increase my business because I shall get more profit; I may increase my benevolence because it ministers more to my pleasure. Thus I have enlarged my life, but I have not enlarged myself; I have moved no nearer to God. Indeed, it is possible for benevolence itself to make us selfish, centring our thoughts more on ourselves, until we admire that which we are doing, when we should be looking up to Him who is the giver of all grace. It is the same with character itself. We may get a knowledge of truth; we may nourish our conscience and our virtuous life, and still not break with that centre; still it may be all for ourselves. To say, " I must be better in order that I may be happier," is as selfish as to say, " I must be richer in order to be happier." Character must look on beyond itself; I must advance, breaking with this little circle, or I have not grown much in character. It is very much the same, strange as it may seem, even with religion. The centre of my religion may still be my heart and my happiness; and as long as I keep it there I have not made any great advance. Indeed, I may pray more, " Lord bless me ; " I may learn to emphasize the " me ; " I may grow willing even to repeat the " me " oftener than I have ; and my prayer be as selfish as it was before, and I not a better man. It is when I can break with this, and look to something beyond, getting another centre for this widening circumference of my life, that I have made an advance.

Thus the call of God here by his prophet to-day is, " Turn you northward. You have compassed this mountain long enough; you have stopped on these things which you are doing and this way of doing things long enough ; you have had this measure of experience long enough; you have been as good as you are quite long enough. Now turn northward." Well, brethren, where is northward? It is an interesting fact, physically, that northward is always up — at least, in all our representations of it — from the time the boy looks to find the north upon his map and finds it at the top of the map, to the time when the man looks up into the heavens for the North Star. Upward, Godward ; that is north. The only north is where the immovable throne of God stands. They tell us that the star which we call the North Star is continually changing, and that the time is coming when the mariner must take another star. The unchanging star which marks the true north is the star which stands over the place where He is enthroned who was the little child beneath the star which led the wise men to his manger.

It is a call of wonderful power, this which tells us that we may go on to something greater than we are. We are to do this; we are to go on nearer to God — nearer to God in our thought, in our purpose, in our life. Or, if that seems too general, we are to go on to that which God has designed for us. It is not very much to say, but it is a stupendous thing to do. We are to fill up the measure of manhood ; not to be gods, not to be angels, but to be men; to do that which we were made to do, the whole of it; to know all that we can know, to do all that we can do, to be all that we can be, going on until we attain unto the measure of the stature of the fulness of the Christ.

In what way does this thought appeal to us this morning? If you will tell me, I will tell you how old you are. If this thought of being a great deal more than you are oppresses you, then you are old, no matter what the family record may say. If you have no thought of going on beyond where you are to-day, then the years are upon you. If, on the other hand, you are receiving with gratification the thought that you can be more; if you feel stirred by it; if already in the midst of this service you find a new purpose coming up; — " I will be more, I will do more in the year to come," your hair may be gray, but you are a young man. The only measure of age is heart, and the measure of heart is hope. When hope is dead, a man is old; when hope is alive, a man is young. So taught the prophet when he said, " They that wait upon the Lord shall renew their strength; they shall mount up with wings as eagles, they shall run and not be weary, they shall walk and not faint." There is something, if we are young enough for it, which is quickening, ennobling, stimulating, and most pleasant to us in this thought. We feel the power of it; we are moved to greater action. There is perhaps no great movement of life which is not toward some great ideal, or under some large influence. To keep the store this year as we did the last is too petty a thing for any man's ambition. To go through the rounds of professional life this year as last, is a dull thing for anybody to do. To read the papers this year as last; to read the same books, or the same kind of books, over and over; to go and come among the same associates, having the same grade of conversation; and to be, when another year ends, uncertain whether it is the end of that year, or the last year, it is dry and hard. No wonder a man says, "Life is vanity of vanities, and what is the use of living?" No wonder men say sometimes under their breath, "I wish I was dead." What is there to live for when there is no hope, and where is the hope if it is not in the thought of being more to-morrow than we are to-day?

The king asked the artist who had taught him to play, and Ole Bull answered, "The mountains of Norway, your Majesty." The mountains of Norway poured their spirit into his willing spirit; the voices of Norway, rolling from its cliffs and sounding from its valleys, whispering in its pines, and murmuring in its seas, ran sounding and thrilling along the strings he touched, until the heart of the world answered to his heart. Who teaches a man to be great? A great thought of God. What makes him diligent in service? I ask a man, and he answers: A great thought of character taught me how much I can be; a magnificent thought of service showed me how much I can do;

I was waked to it; I was summoned by it; I heard it in God's providence; I listened to it in God's house; that I might break with myself,— break the very centre of my life; that I might push on to higher employments and greater accomplishments; that I might have a more profound and blessed experience. When I heard God say how great I might be, and how great things I might do for him; how large a manhood I might fulfil and how much of divinity I might possess, then the "mountains of Norway" taught me to live, and I live in the life that evermore grows into the stature of the divine fulness. It was thus that St. Paul became great. It was a continual enlargement of his life. Not content with treading the streets of Tarsus, from school to school, he pressed his way to Jerusalem; not satisfied with the added schools of Jerusalem, or to wander through the intricacies and subtilties of Hebrew jurisprudence, he pressed on his way still, keeping all of good which he had learned, until he heard God's voice before the gate of Damascus: "O, Saul, Saul, thou hast trodden this petty round long enough; turn northward;" and he went out to that magnificent career. It was so with Moses. After his long years in Pharaoh's palace, going round within the halls, he pressed on into the wilderness; he was forty years in the wilderness keeping sheep, until at last the voice of God came to him, speaking out of the bush that burned and was not consumed, "Thou hast compassed this mountain long enough, turn northward;" and he went down to become one of the leading statesmen of the world. It was so with our Lord's disciples; fishermen from their youth, fishing this year quite as well as last, next year as well as this, until the voice of the Lord found them: "Simon, son of Jonas, John, James, Andrew, Thomas — you have compassed the Sea of Galilee with your boats long enough: turn northward, follow me and I will make you fishers." — "But, Lord, we are already fishermen; we do not think we can learn skill in fishing from a carpenter." "Follow me, and I will make you fishers of men; turn northward, beyond the Sea of Galilee, beyond the fish that swim in their multitudes through its depths, and you shall gather men."

This is the summons of Christ to us. The beginning of it must be as we hear his voice, and answer to it — Christ's voice, calling and inspiring us for higher and holier things. If any one asks "What am I to do?" there is always but one answer; "You are to begin, and to begin as you ought to begin." One great reason why we never advance wisely, is because we never begin wisely.

Begin with God; give yourself to God here, to Christ here. "Lord, I take thee," that is right. "I take thee for my Saviour," that is one thing never to be given up. "I take thee for my Master," — that is an endless beginning; then in obedience to him, press on. "I love him, I serve him, I follow where he leads me." It is thus that we go on to a high and holy living, and to the eternal reward.

There are one or two thoughts touching this life that we are living which I should like to add to what I have already said. We need to-day, perhaps we need every day, to get a juster view of life. We are very familiar with it, and yet how little we know about it. It is such a simple thing to live, to keep going and coming, and coming and going. More rational, intelligent views of life will certainly very greatly change our lives. We ought to look upon life as full of opportunity. We say we are entering upon a new year, and a new year is a great thing. I know how brief a year seems as we look back upon it; but there is a great deal of time in a year. It is most superficial to say that a year is a very small piece of life; it is a large piece of life. Three hundred days and more; three hundred days wherein we can be making our will stronger for God; three hundred days in which we can be doing good in the world; serving Christ, loving Christ; three hundred days with their hours over God's word, in the closet and in the sanctuary; three hundred days with their Sabbaths for the church, and the ministry and the work of the church! Why, it is a grand thing, a sublime thing to have so much time. Time is to be regarded as opportunity; not as something which we are to receive simply as a matter with which we have nothing to do, but to let it come to us as the wind comes blowing about us. We are to take it rather as the wind comes to the sailor who finds he has a use for it; who cares very much whether the wind blows or not, and which way it blows. They tell us sometimes that life is like a stream. It seems a very apt comparison, these years are passing on so rapidly. But we are not to stand upon the bank of this stream and look out upon it, and think of the waves, and the rapidity of the current, and whither the waters are hurrying so fast. We are to feel that we are to enter upon this stream and to use it. We are not to be taken up by it, as the stream takes up the tree which has fallen upon its bank and carries it on whithersoever it will. We are not to go upon it as the raft goes, a few timbers hastily fastened together to last a few days until something else shall be found, or we shall strike some island beyond. We are not to go upon it as the boat goes, simply to be drifted down as the tide runs; nor as the ferryboat, which sails equally well in all directions, and, with a continual movement, never makes much of a voyage. I think we are rather to go as the ship goes, which looses from its moorings and turns its prow towards the distant port, with a strong hand at the helm, the chart spread out and the compass lighted day and night, while it seeks boldly its way across the wide seas to its appointed haven.

They tell us that life is a vapor. So it is. That means more than it did when St. James wrote the word. Almost the mightiest force in the world to-day is vapor. Condense it, heat it, and it makes the ship fly from shore to shore. Put it in its place, and it turns the ponderous machinery of the factory and clothes the land. Life is vapor; thin, transparent; passing away into the clouds. The good man's life is vapor held, heated, used; made a power that makes the world move. The value of life is to be found in what we do with it. As I have intimated already, the measure of life is in that which we do in life. There is nothing that is more futile and deceptive than the attempt to measure life by years. It was one of the profound remarks of a wise man, that "Time is not the measure of life, but life is the measure of time." He taught the students how to make the sun stand still by putting the work of two days into one. "By crowding the year with generous purposes, virtuous efforts and noble sacrifices." The only hours of the last year which are of much account are those in which we advanced; the moments in which we moved forward; the days in which we learned something; the days in which you did something are the real time. The rest has vanished like the morning cloud.

Do I ask, then, that there may come to us a higher and a holier life, and that there may be taken upon us more work and better work? I know the response at once; that we are overworked already. The answer is too easily made. It is somewhat significant that the men who talk the most about our overwork, do not appear to be very much overworked themselves. It is the overwork of somebody else, usually, which they are talking about. It is too often the case that the people who are afraid of too much work are those who are fond of their beds. I do not find the best working men of our day complaining that there is too much to do, and that men are wearing out too fast. They believe that God gives a man strength for duty, and that when a man can no longer work, he has no longer any need to live. God gives us what we can do, and we are to take it and do it. Still, are we not very busy, are we not engaged every moment, so that there seems no room to put in anything else? Very likely; I think it is so with most of us; but I do not see that this has much to do with the question before us. Suppose we do not enlarge the volume of our work, but only the character of it. Can you not drop some things which you are doing and take on better things? St. Paul said, "When I was a child, I thought as a child, I spake as a child;" but when he became a man, he found that he had not room enough for childish things and manly things too, and he gave up childish things, and took on those which suited his years. When he was to run a race, he forgot the things which were behind; he put off the things that troubled and beset him; not because his raiment was not good, but because he could not run with it. I have no doubt that every one of us is carrying many things which are taking up his time, but which he might well enough let alone, because he has outgrown them. What are the engrossing demands of my life, is a simple question for every one to ask. Are there not things which have taken hours of the last year for which we are too old, which we ought to have left behind us while we turned to something better; things which somebody else who was younger, who had not been taught of God so long, could do just as well? I think that it is so, and I believe that we can be continually dropping the easier and the smaller things to our children, to young men and to young women, while we take up those which are more fitting our years, and go on and do them steadfastly to the end. The glory of our life will be just there; it is when we do something we have never done before, and something better than we have done before, that we are making an advance.

It was asked concerning a great artist once, "Wherein is it that he excels?" The reply was, "He begins where other people end." We cannot all do that, for there are some men who never seem to end their advance. But every man can begin where he himself had ended. We can begin where we have already stopped. There is something more which we can do for the world; something more for God; something more for our own life. It may require giving up some things which are taking our time; but our vows to the Church, and our duties in the Church, and our duties to God and to the world, we can meet by laying aside the poorer things for the better ones; by compassing the mountain no longer; by taking up that which is real and pressing our way forward.

This is my greeting to-day. Once again do I wish you sincerely a "Happy New Year." Perhaps we have compassed these words long enough. Let me put my wish into other words; and they shall be two sentences from two great men. The one speaks the word of God out of the Old Scriptures, and the other out of the New. This, brethren beloved, is my wish for the New Year:

"Ye have compassed this mountain long enough; turn you northward."

"If ye then be risen with Christ, seek those things which are above."

X.

WHAT MUST I DO?

SCRIPTURE LESSON : *Acts* viii : 26–40.
TEXT : What must I do to be saved ? *Acts* xvi: 30.

IT is a question of interest to us all. It concerns any who are not saved; it concerns all who are saved, because it is our duty to save others. The question asked in a prison has been repeated through the world. The answer joined to it has gained nothing, lost nothing, as the years have passed by, and it has done its work of mercy, "blessing him who gives and him who takes." There is but one answer to the question. The apostle and his companion had been pursuing their work in Philippi, that Macedonian, Grecian, Roman city. They had stirred up the anger of the people and the avarice of those who were gaining gold by an unlawful service. They had been seized by the mob, dragged to the market-place and delivered to the magistrates, who stripped them of their robes, beat them with rods, and committed them to the care of the jailer who thrust them into the inner prison and made their feet fast in the stocks. At midnight they prayed and sang their praises unto God. They sang, as it were, a "new song;" it was new to them, for this was a new experience. They sang one of the songs in the night. The book of Psalms, with which they were familiar from their childhood, abounds in hymns which would be appropriate at such a time. We are at a loss to know what they selected for their worship and prayer. It may be that they sang the song of Asaph, as it is in the seventy-ninth Psalm : "Let the sighing of the prisoner come before thee; according to the greatness of thy power preserve thou those who are appointed to die." The prisoners were hearing them, and the Lord heard them; and the prison walls were shaken and the doors opened; every man's bands were loosed; and the keeper awoke and drew his sword, and would have killed himself had not the apostle preserved his life; when the man, calling for lights, plunged into the darkness which had been bright enough for better men, and, falling at the feet of his captives, said, "Lords, what must I do to be saved?" "Believe on the Lord," answered St. Paul, "and thou shalt be saved." And he believed and committed himself to God's mercy; he listened to the word of the apostle; he was baptized; he washed the stripes of his prisoners; "he set meat before them, and rejoiced, believing in God with all his house."

It was a famous place. On the broad plains of Philippi had been fought the battle upon whose issue hung the empire of the world. There Brutus and Cassius had sought to restore the commonwealth, building it on the bleeding corse of Cæsar. There the dream of a republic had ended, and Roman liberty had itself been slain. It is not strange that in that defeat, that destruction of all his hopes, the last of the Romans killed himself by the hand of his freedman, and that Brutus fell on Strato's sword. The evil genius of Brutus, which had promised aforetime to meet him at Philippi, had met him there, and there had come the final destruction of his hope. The only remedy for despair was suicide. It is not strange that this jailer, familiar with this remedy of greater men in their desperation, sought through the gate which it opened deliverance from the terrors which environed him. But a better genius than that of Brutus was there. The apostle of Christ was there; the Spirit of God was there, in the heart of the apostle, in the heart of the jailer; and it meant not death, but life; not defeat, but victory. His character and his hope were erected into the stately fabric of everlasting life.

We are impressed here with the temperate manner of the greatest of men; with the calmness of his demeanor; with the masterful spirit which is in him. This is the same man who, a little later, kept a frightened ship's crew in subjection, and controlled the soldiers who were carrying him to his death. This man, with the prison doors opened and the prisoners startled and ready to flee, in all the tumult of that midnight hour held them, we may believe, by the dignity of his presence, by the authority of his voice, by the supremacy of his will, asserting that manhood, which, though cast down, is not destroyed, and when thrown into perplexity never sinks into despair; wearing that royalty which nothing can take away; the royalty wherewith he had been crowned by Him who makes men kings and priests.

> Not all the water in the rough rude sea,
> Can wash the balm from an annointed king.

This question of the jailer was admirably put. We can hardly imagine the various constituents which must enter into such an inquiry better arranged than in these words which were driven from him in the excitement of that hour. He had brought the question to the right place. He might have searched the world over and never found a man to whom the question could be so fittingly addressed as it came from the heart which asked it to the heart which could answer it. How common experiences bring us to a level! What matter what one's age, or estate, or condition in life, in a sinking ship, in a burning house, a shattered prison; in the presence of God, Jehovah of hosts! It was but seventeen years before, when the man who heard this question, himself affrighted, thrown to the ground, confronted with the Lord who stood before this jailer, uttered the same inquiry. What Saul of Tarsus had asked at the gate of Damascus, this jailer asked within the prison of Philippi. What the Lord had answered to Saul of Tarsus, the Lord answered to the jailer; and he who had spoken to the apostle, gave him the grace to repeat the answer which needed no enlargement, which falls with all its power from human lips, because it is the word of the Christ, and not the man. This man was able to repeat that which had come to him, and to point his brother, his fellow-sinner, to the redemption which had availed for him, and which, through the years since, he had been ministering unto others, as he was to do through the years to come, until he laid his head upon the block. It is one of the instructive coincidences of Holy Scripture, that a question which Saul of Tarsus had asked so long before, and whose answer he had received and acted upon ever afterwards, should be asked of him by this Pagan, and should be answered by him as it was answered to him, "an Hebrew of the Hebrews." There is but one answer. He who would be saved must believe on the Lord Jesus-Christ. The eternities shall roll away, but that direction will remain; and no man shall be saved, but by the grace of God which is in Jesus Christ his Son. Who to-day intrusts himself to it, to-day is saved.

But the question itself, if we separate it word

from word, brings together those elements which should enter into the inquiry: "What must I do;" not these prisoners, not the rulers, not the emperor; "what must I do?" One has not come seriously to look at any duty until he stands alone with God. I have not seen my duty until I have seen it as my duty, and do not know other men in it. "What must I do?" Not what should I prefer to do; but what is it necessary that I should do? Among the divine and everlasting truths of God which move on forever, what is the way to which I *must* conform my life, if I would be saved? "What must I do?" Not, in what way may I drift into life? Not, how long may I live before, like a broken ship thrown upon the waves, I am dashed upon some island in the sea? Not, when shall the mercy of God, without any covenant, through the slow wearing on of the ages, move me into salvation? What must *I do* in order that I may be saved? "What must I do *to be saved?*" Not, to save myself, but *to be* saved; to come into that condition in which I shall be saved by another, — I, who cannot save myself.

With what force this man asks this question. It seems a strange inquiry to come from such a man, at such a time, with such surroundings. It is very plain that he did not mean, " What shall I do to be saved from this terror, this present peril?" He knew the rigor of Roman law. But surely he could not feel himself to blame because there had been an earthquake shaking the prison. He could not accuse himself of deserting his trust, for his prisoners were all there. If there were anything to result from that excitement it would seem to be his advancement. A jailer who, under those circumstances, could keep his prisoners safe, and the next morning show them to the authorities, might expect promotion under the government, if promotion follows merit. But he had seen God and was troubled; what should he do?

This word salvation had become familiar in Philippi. A damsel, filled with a spirit of divination, day by day had followed Paul and Silas as they went to prayer, and cried out after them with the spirit of a prophetess, "These men are the servants of the most high God, which show unto us the way of salvation, and this did she many days." Day after day, "salvation," "salvation;" "which show unto us the way of salvation," went ringing along the streets of Philippi until St. Paul commanded the spirit to come out of her. Then her masters caused her deliverers to be beaten and imprisoned. It may be that this man had heard the frenzied girl. He knew what she had said. He saw the men whom she followed, and her masters accused, rescued by their God, when he had made their feet fast in the stocks. Salvation as a word had become familiar to him. In the presence of God it became a necessity as a fact. We are not to think of this man as rough and rude beyond his fellows. Doubtless he was of good repute. He would not have been intrusted with so responsible a position as this, in a place of so great account, had he not been a man of intelligence and honesty and ability. He had not beaten Paul and Silas; he had thrust them into the inner prison because he was so commanded. There is no sign of any harshness on his part towards them, save as he obeyed the orders of his superiors. What is a man to do when the court delivers a prisoner to his keeping, but to obey the behest of the court. May we not think, too, that this man, intelligent as he was, who seems, as he appears at last as the head of a family, to have had those gentler qualities which commend our common human nature, perhaps had the thought of God in his mind before? There has been found now and then — sad that it has been so seldom — a man among the heathen in whom God has kept his witness; who has the thought of God, who has the desire for a better life, who would fain be at peace with him who rules in the armies of heaven and among the inhabitants of the earth. There is no intimation that this was such a man. But it is clear that he knew that the great God was there in the prison. He had come to rescue his men. What should the jailer do in the presence of one at whose tread the stones rattled in the wall?

Plainly there was but one thing for him to do, and that was what the apostles pointed out to him. "What must I do to be saved" from this God who is here; this God of power, in whose hands I am? You are reminded of that incident in St. Peter's life when, brought face to face with the power of God, and startled by the miracle of Christ, feeling his own unworthiness, afraid to stand in such a presence, he cried, "Depart from me; for I am a sinful man, O Lord." "For he was astonished, and all that were with him." This man was amazed, and affrighted; he saw God and his might. God was there, shaking the very foundations of his prison, and taking his prisoners out of his hand. He was afraid; afraid in the presence of the Almighty, whose breath might remove him from the earth.

Now, what answer must the apostle give to a question like this? "What shall I do that I may be saved and brought into the favor of God who is here?" There is but one answer. If this man is to be saved, he must in some way become right with God. He must submit his life to God, and enter the company of those who obey him and on whom his approval rests and abides forever. The apostle summoned him to God. Let us mark the simplicity of that which the apostle said. He called the man to the obedience of God. We often discuss this question of salvation on side issues, and oftentimes very blindly.

We reason as if God is there, with his justice and law, and Christ is here with his redemption; so that if one has gone away from God and disobeyed him, he must find the mercy of Christ and trust himself to that. But where are righteousness and piety on this plan? The apostle called this man back to God himself. He must submit to God and take up his duty from the hands of God. There is no salvation without that. But if he comes to God, in what attitude shall he find him? Must he come to the law-giver? But he had broken the commands. Must he come to a God who is simply almighty? But that power was likely to destroy him. If he found favor with God at all, it must be because God was merciful towards him. God in mercy is the God whom he must find. First he must find God; secondly, he must find God in mercy, willing to forgive and to restore; willing to take him into his service again; and thirdly, having found God in mercy, he must take up the commands of God and go steadfastly and patiently on, doing the will of God.

May I repeat these three things? This man, if he is to be saved, must come to God, and give himself to him. Secondly, he must come to God as he is in mercy; and thirdly, he must come to God in mercy to render to him the obedience and devotion of his life. Why, then, did the apostle say, "Believe on the Lord Jesus Christ?"

Because the Lord Jesus Christ is the mercy of God. The name of God's mercy on the earth is Christ. That fine line of Faber may come to your mind:

<blockquote>Jesus, God's love, is crucified.</blockquote>

This is mercy. God's love beyond the heavens can do nothing for us unless it reaches where we are; and when God's love reaches where we are it is mercy; and God's mercy where we are is named Jesus Christ, his Son. You find the mercy when you find him; you find him when you find the mercy.

Let us then feel that this answers the question; that we come into the mercy of God as it is in Christ Jesus our Lord; and then, having come into the mercy, we take our duty from Christ's lips and go on to follow him to the end.

Dropping all that is local and temporal, passing away from Philippi and its prison which has become the school for so many penitent hearts, we will notice these things, which have no limitation of time or of place, but which come in all their reality to us to-day. What must a man do to be saved? Suffer me to answer it once more as I have already. A man to be saved, must come into the approval of God. When God says you are right, then you are saved; as long as God says you are wrong, you are lost. When God's mercy covers you, you are saved; when you are without that mercy, you are lost. When you are doing God's will, you are saved; when it is not the law of your life to do God's will, you are lost. There is no salvation for a man except in doing the will of God; and "he that doeth the will of God abideth forever." This is the essential thing.

When the thought is borne in upon us, as it often is, that there must be something done for our salvation, there are three courses which we may take. The first course, and perhaps the rarer, is despair. "There is no hope, no; for I have loved strangers, and after them will I go." One may say, "I have done wrong and there is no forgiveness for me; I am surrounded by the world, I am entangled in its toils; there is no help for me." I think that is not very common. A second course, much more common, perhaps more perilous, is to attempt, by some sort of compromise, to effect that which can only be effected by obedience. This method is old. Mr. Froude says, that when religion had subsided to an opinion at Rome, the people built more elegant temples than ever, and devoted themselves more scrupulously to the ceremonial. It has been quite a common experience, that, when faith has declined, a regard for the forms of religion, and for the external duties which it enjoins, has increased; men who have broken with God and will not return to him, take up, as a compromise, the doing of certain things which all acknowledge to be excellent, in the hope that this may be accepted in the place of obedience. That is, when I owe you money and will not pay you, if I am kind to your children, you will forgive me the debt. When I have a note at your bank, and, with money in my hands, refuse to pay it, if in other respects I am well-behaved, you will send me my note cancelled when it becomes due. If I am amiable and pleasant among men, that will balance my lack of integrity. Is this a caricature? I see something like it every day. Men say when this thought of unrighteousness is pressed home upon them, "I will try to do better; I will read my Bible more." But reading the Bible is not fully obeying God. "I will attend church more faithfully." But attending church is not obeying God. "I will be more careful about my prayers." But being careful about your prayers is not obeying God. "I will try to be more gentle and kind and friendly with men." Admirable! But being all this is not obeying God. This is on a lower plane, and is no substitute for the obedience of God. It is only by doing God's will that a man ever can have life; and one is grieved to the heart when he finds that men are trying to substitute good wishes and prayers and reading the Bible and attending church and speaking well of religion, for the simple-hearted obedience of God. I would not speak lightly — Oh, that I might speak with more than human eloquence of the value of virtue and morality in the earth! I would exalt reading the Bible and prayer and the reverence of God in the sanctuary, and honor and sincerity and truthfulness among men. All these God requires. But when all this is done, it may be that we have not found God. It was the shrewd and sharp saying of some one upon the "Charge of the Six Hundred," when they rushed "into the jaws of death, into the mouth of hell," throwing away their lives to accomplish nothing, "This is magnificent, but it is not war." Something like that may be said of all the forms of virtue and decorum: "These are magnificent, but they are not religion." There is no religion without God, and a man is not religious until he thinks of God. Morality is not religious until a man is moral because God requires it, and he renders his morality to him. The circle must have a centre, or it is not a circle; and the centre of religion is God. The needle of the compass must find the north; and the north of morality is God. When morality points to him, then it is religion. Why should we not do right to please God, and for his sake possess the virtues? Why should we think that adorning the prison and softening the fetters and loosening the stocks for men is a worthy substitute for the belief on the Lord Jesus Christ which alone can save man?

We can come to this thought of the necessity of our submitting ourselves to God in obedience, if we think upon the relation which we are to bear to him forever. We might, perhaps, otherwise come into a state in which we should be reasonably content, if it were not for the fact that God is love. Friends, I do not know how it impresses you, but the most serious truth which I have to confront in questions of duty is that God is love. I should have an easier conscience if it were not for that. I should care less for his treatment of me, if he did not love me. It is little to you that the stranger on the street does not notice you; but if your friend passes you by! It is little to this man that the boys do not speak to him; but if his own children will not speak to him! It is a small matter to the boys that the men whom they meet do not smile upon them; but if their father or mother will not look kindly on them! I can think of nothing which shall be harder for the lost than to see the averted face of the love of God. To look at him from the golden streets, while I walk beneath the trees which yield their fruit every month; to look up to God and find him turning away; and to think that he cannot look approvingly upon me, but that I am spending my years under his disapproval, knowing that he is dissatisfied with me, displeased with my motives, discontented with my life, might well make me desire to depart from heaven and be at peace.

The man was not driven away by the soldiers, nor by the girl who frightened him. He stood his ground; he kept by the fire and warmed himself, that Galilean fisherman. But at last, when no one was speaking, no hand was uplifted, no threat had reached him, suddenly this stout man went out, and in the darkness wept bitterly, for "the Lord turned and looked upon Peter." The hardest look to bear is the sorrowful look of a friend. His anger you could endure, but his sorrow crushes the heart. "Peter went out" — of course he went out. The world was not wide enough to give him a place where he could stand and bear the sight of those sorrowful eyes. The years were not brief enough for him to pass through them and lose sight of that tearful, pleading gaze, when "the Lord turned and looked upon Peter." How could a man live forever under the sad eyes, and before the broken heart of the only friend he ever had? Call it heaven, if you will, but do not call it blessedness. There is no salvation until Christ smiles upon us; until God approves us. When God is pleased, we are saved; when God is contented, we are right; when the face of the Son of God looks approvingly upon us, here in these streets, or yonder in the celestial courts, we are in heaven.

Brethren, I am not speaking to-day of the delights of Paradise. I am asking simply this: that you and I may be right. Let us once for all be done with the delusion that God is so good we may wrong him, and that because God is love it does not matter what he thinks of us. We *do* care what he thinks of us; and we care all the more, and we shall always care the more, because God is love. There is nothing that persuades me more into the necessity that I must be right if I would find heaven, than that God's love summons me to this obedience.

This is the word which God's Spirit brings to us this morning. We must regard this question which is before us. Let us be right in the righteousness of it. Our duty is plain. Shall we do it? We shall be saved when God knows that the secret spring of our life is true to him. That was a fine sentence in one of the papers last week. Some one, writing of Mr. Gladstone, who had been obliged to give up a visit to his constituents on account of his health, said, "When Mr. Gladstone says that he regards it as an obligation to have an interview with the electors of Midlothian, that is the same thing as saying it will be performed." That, I suppose, may be taken as the leading characteristic of the grandest Englishman of our day. It makes any life grand, and any life is feeble without it. To see that a thing ought to be done, and to have this equivalent to seeing that it is done, makes up a heroic life. We see our duty; we confess it. Is that the pledge that we will do it?

I plead to-day simply for the right. A man ought to love God. Shall we submit our life to God? We must come to God's mercy, because we are guilty. The mercy of God is Jesus Christ, his Son. There before this incarnate, redeeming mercy, we will say, "Here, Lord, I give myself away. I take thy will and it shall govern me; I take thy word, and it shall teach me." "But shall I not fail? How can I know the will of God?" one asks. He shall guide you into all truth. "How can I do the will of God?" He shall keep you from falling, and present you faultless before the presence of his glory with exceeding joy. "Can I come up out of this inconstant and guilty life into the grace of God, forever to abide within his compassion?" "The Spirit and the Bride say, come;" and the mercy of God saith "Come, all ye that labor and are heavy laden; Come unto me, for I am God's mercy, and I will give you rest."

Three things, then, beloved: First, to devote our life from this hour steadfastly unto obedience to God; secondly, to intrust ourselves steadfastly unto God in mercy, which is Christ; thirdly, from this hour to go our way doing those things which will please Christ.

I leave this word with you with these sentences of Holy Scripture, which teach us that, if a man return to God he shall be saved; that, if a man out of his broken life will come back and begin life again at the mercy of God, he shall be saved; and that the power that shall save him is the mercy of God in Jesus Christ his Son.

"This is a faithful saying, and worthy of all acceptation, that Jesus Christ came into the world to save sinners."

" There is none other name under heaven given among men, whereby we must be saved."

" He is able to save them to the uttermost that come unto God by him."

" The blood of Jesus Christ his Son cleanseth us from all sin."

" The precious blood of Christ."

XI.

THE LOVE OF GOD MANIFESTED.

SCRIPTURE LESSON : *I John.* Chapter iv.

TEXT: In this was manifested the love of God toward us, because that God sent his only begotten Son into the world, that we might live through him. Herein is love; not that we loved God, but that he loved us, and sent his Son to be the propitiation for our sins. *I John* iv: 9 and 10.

WE may add to this the fourteenth verse: "We have seen and do testify that the Father sent the Son to be the Saviour of the world." There is, then, a grand truth which lies before all which God, our Father, has done for us, in the love which he has for us. God is love, and God loves us. There can be no question more important than this: What is the feeling of God towards men, as they are really living and working in the world? The answer of our Lord is, that when men needed to be saved, God loved the world.

We have this precedent fact of the love of God; we have the love of God giving his Son for men; we have the love of God following the gift of his

Son with those calls which bid us to eternal life.
When we read the story of Christ's life as it is
written in the Old Scriptures, we find this movement of God's love through all his work and
in his words. God is seen reasoning with men,
bidding them to reason with him, though their
sins be as scarlet; calling them to himself, though
they are going away to death — " Turn ye, turn
ye, for why will ye die?" God is found talking
with himself and calling himself to account, lest
in anything his love has come short; going as the
vine-dresser among his vines, looking up through
the leaves and parting them here and there, that
he may see if anywhere there is a ripened cluster;
at last dropping his hands in despair and crying
out in that sad and anxious sentence, "What
could have been done more to my vineyard, that I
have not done in it?" We are to lay this down
as the grand truth; the grand fact never to be
questioned — against which our reasoning and our
feeling are never to prevail; which nothing in
law or judgment is to destroy — the love that
God has for men; for men in their guilt,
for men in their death. We are able to repeat, and, with our voice rising as we say the
words, we do repeat those spirited lines of the
English preacher and singer, when he seems
to throw all his force into his song, lest some one
should question it, or as if somewhere he had
heard some whisper of doubt concerning it:

> I say to thee, do thou repeat
> To the first man thou mayest meet,
> In lane, highway, or open street —
> That he, and we, and all men move
> Under a canopy of Love
> As broad as the blue sky above.

* * * * * * *

> And one thing further make him know,
> That to believe these things are so,
> This firm faith never to forego —
> Despite of all which seems at strife
> With blessing, and with curses rife —
> That this *is* blessing, this *is* life.

From this fact of God's love, pass now to the manifesting of God's love; for it is obvious that if it be love it must show itself. A mere emotion beyond the heavens, in the breast of God, avails us nothing. It is not love unless it lives. There is no such thing as dead love, and "They never loved who dream that they loved once." God's love must move because it is living; it must seek those towards whom it looks, that it may bless them out of its own wealth and strength.

An Italian writer not long ago, speaking of one of the most famous of modern Spanish painters, whose works he had been examining, said, "It is the last point which painting can reach before being translated into action." The painter could only drop his brush and do the things which he had depicted; that was all which was beyond; but that was a wonderful thing beyond. It is a great step from the thought to the deed; from the man upon the canvas to the man upon the street; from the love looking from out the painted eyes to the love dropping from out the living hands. God's love coming from the divine eternal repose into a life wherewith it seeks to bring men to itself, this is love doing the one thing which makes love perfect.

God's love shows itself to men before Christ comes. It is in his favor and his providence; it is in his long-suffering patience, and compassion; it is in his exceeding great and precious promises; it is in his communion with men, bearing them up as a shepherd bears his sheep; carrying them as an eagle carries her young; keeping them as one keeps the flock in the green pastures and by the still waters. God's love moves through all. It is in great events; when he calls Abraham to be the leader of humanity; when he raises Moses from the bulrushes to be the world's lawgiver; when he sends the prophets to instruct the world in morals and religion, until he whose day the prophets heralded shall come. This is the love of God.

But all this has not availed to accomplish God's purposes. On the night when Christ was born, the world did not know that Jehovah was God. A few Jews in Jerusalem and Juda, and scattered here and there through the lands, knew; but the world in its despair bowed before its idols, and Paganism itself was breaking to its fall.

There was one thing more that God could do. He could come into the world himself; not send, but come. We are brought, then, to the thought which the apostle here presents to us as we gather up these teachings to-day with the other teachings out of the heart of this same man, who was " that disciple whom Jesus loved," and we see God's love alive, in the world, at its best and doing its best for men. It seems a singular thing as we make up the merit of men, and the desert of actions, that this which is done by the Son of God in the earth, with which we are familiar, should be ascribed to God. I think it almost the strangest verse in the Bible, when you take it by itself, that which St. Paul wrote to the Romans: "God commendeth his love toward us, in that Christ died for us." I ask you to admire my patriotism and devotion, for I know a man who went out and died for his country. You say, " I should think it was that man's devotion which was to be admired, rather than yours." God commendeth his love because somebody else died for us. One would think it should be that Christ commendeth his love because he died for us. I could readily understand that; the other is not so clear. But you say it is marvellous love when God gives his Son to the world that he may bear our burdens, and suffer and die for us. That is true. But does not the chief love belong to him who comes? Is it love which, taking sorrow from us, lays it upon another? We may call it loving us, but what will the Son say? We may call it a manifestation of love on the one hand helping *us*; what shall we say of that on the other hand, crushing *him?*

I have no solution of this mystery, except that which our Lord himself gave, which was this: "I and my Father are one. The Son can do nothing of himself." He was so thoroughly one with the Father, that he could not think, or love, or act apart from him. They could not be separated. The love of the Son was the love of God. I see, then, how God may commend his love when the Son of God dies, for the Father and the Son are one. God comes to us, enters into our humanity, loving us and putting his love into exercise for us, under this name of the Son; under the name of Jesus the Saviour; under that other name Immanuel, which is, being interpreted by him who alone can interpret his names; who alone can translate his life into our thought: which is, being interpreted, "God with us."

"O Lamb of God, was ever pain, was ever love like thine!"

We have, then, these facts: we have Christ giving himself for us; God sending his Son, as the Scripture teaches; Christ coming into the world, as he said of himself, and thus redeeming us; giving himself, as the text says this morning, first as "the propitiation for our sins;" secondly, "that we might live through him;" and thirdly, as it is described in that larger phrase, "to be the Saviour of the world."

We are not to look upon this act of God in giving his son as a singular act, separate from the whole spirit of his life; a new law which has entered into the world. Christ is but fulfilling an eternal law in this, that he gives himself for men. There are three expressions to which I will call your attention particularly now, that you may see how this life of Christ in the world is carrying out a grand, broad principle which is working all the time among men. This law has three statements. First, it is in this, and it is Christ's statement: "Except a corn of wheat fall into the ground and die, it abideth alone"; but if it give up its life, if it die, then other grains, and many grains, spring from it, and it is glorified in this multiplying and ennobling of its life. The second statement is this: "I am the bread of life;" ye are to eat this bread and live forever. Bread is this grain of wheat sprung up and multiplied; and then this new grain is itself bruised, crushed, made into bread, which, again, is of no service until it is dead. No; not until you consume the bread does it do you any good. But when the bread has given itself for you, then it enters into your virtue and knowledge; into the immortality which comes here in its beginning. It becomes a part of you. It is not a poor loaf upon the shelf, but its strength is in you, that you may live by means of it. The third and only other illustration which I will mention, is this: "I am the good shepherd;" I am "come to seek and to save that which was lost," as the shepherd goes after the one sheep which has wandered from the ninety and nine; goes up into the cold mountain, finds him, and brings him down into the fold at his own cost. Nay, "I am the good shepherd," who, finding the sheep in great peril, throws himself between the sheep and the peril, and gives his life for the sheep. Then the sheep live, and he lives in them. For Christ rising from the dead becomes more than ever the shepherd of the sheep; receiving more from them in their affection and their service, while he is glorified in that which he has done for them. There is, perhaps, no more vivid portraiture of the work of Christ than this, as he paints it out upon the Judan background; the sheep and the wolves, and the Christ between. It is a strong picture and full of meaning. But there is one thing more than the beauty of the words; it is the beauty of the deed, when the living Christ gives his life for the sheep.

We have considered the fact and the method; shall we look now at the reason of the fact? Why is it that Christ gives himself for the sheep? Why is it that, being the bread of life, he consents to be eaten? Why is it that, being the grain of living wheat, he consents to die?

First, he does not die because he is guilty. We associate suffering with guilt. He is not guilty; he is holy. He does not die because he is weak. He is three and thirty years old, and all his strength is in him; he has a multitude attending him; he has the world open before him; yet he goes steadfastly to the cross. He does not die because he is compelled. If he does, there is no patriot soldier who does not exceed him in devotion. "I lay down my life of myself; no man taketh it from me." He does not die, again, because he is under obligation; it is his free and gracious act. He does not die reluctantly; he talked but little of his dying, though in that little he said wonderful things. When Jesus came to his death he said this: "The hour is come, that the Son of man should be glorified." It was the glory of dying to redeem, which, in his thought, surpassed the death itself.

Or, again, to change the list a little; he does not come into the world and give himself for men because God is angry with men, and needs to be persuaded and appeased; for even then God loves men. He does not die for men because he is bearing their punishment, being himself holy. No one can bear the punishment of another. Guilt cannot be transferred, and no man can be punished for anything but his own offences. He does not give himself for men because there is a deficiency in that which God has done which he wishes to fill out; because of a sudden purpose of love springing up in God's mind. The love of God was in his law, making every syllable of it, as truly as it was in his redemption, bringing men back to it. He does not die, fourthly, that he may reconcile justice and mercy. God's justice is merciful and God's mercy is just. It is reconciling a thing unto itself to speak of reconciling the two sides of the one thought of God. Neither, finally, does he die as if this were his last estate, simply to perish, one more victim, one more man giving himself that others may live while he remains dead. He gives himself to rise from the grave, and to bear humanity redeemed up into his own glory, and to live and reign forever where the saints of God render their homage and their worship unto him who sitteth upon the throne and unto the Lamb.

I am asked, then, passing from these negative considerations, why it is that God's love takes this especial form. We notice these three things: In the first place, that men need to be saved. Secondly, that Christ could save men if he would. Thirdly, that Christ loves men enough to save them. Men need, Christ is able, Christ is willing; there you have the atonement. You need it; it is possible for it to become real. There is love enough to make it real. The whole truth is comprehended in those three statements. We are standing upon holy ground. Men have formed upon these facts various explanations, and some of them are admirable. It is good to see how vigorous and glowing are the thoughts of men touching this fact of the redeeming love of Christ. They have studied it, turned it to the light, sought the reason for it, followed out the methods of its working, and made to themselves the plans in which all the parts find a place. Their studies make excellent reading. Yet it will be noticed that in these explanations there is one simple truth. From different ways of looking at life, men come to different conclusions upon almost every subject. There is this noteworthy thing in regard to the various studies upon the redemption of Christ, that, however men may pursue the theme, they come back to one great truth. From the highest sacrificial theory which makes Christ bear the burden of our guilt, to the humbler idea which makes him simply one who appeals to our conscience and affection, they agree in this substantial and central fact: that Christ gave himself to save men, and that because Christ gave himself, men can be saved. With many points of difference they agree in that. It is very instructive that the study of the history of Christ's life, as it is recorded in the Scriptures, shows him as the shepherd between the sheep and the wolves.

If we can see Christ in that position, we have seen the very heart of it all. If we can understand this, and receive it heartily, we have received Christ as he gives himself for men.

I delight to read what men say about this. Often have I read it, patiently have I studied it. I shall continue to read with an open mind. But I always come back to the New Testament, and always must do so, for it is there alone that I find the explanation of Christ's work which satisfies me. I am deeply impressed with the conviction that if there is any privilege which should be accorded to everybody, it is the privilege of telling why he does a thing. I claim that right. My action may be foolish; it may seem to you irrational; but I assert my right as against the world, to explain my conduct. What I ask for myself I give to others; and most of all to the Christ of God. To him belongs the right to tell why he came into the world, why he gave his life for men, what he expected to accomplish by the offering of himself, what he thinks men ought to do to avail themselves of it. I come back from my rambling to say, " O my Saviour, thou hast the right to give thine own account of thy life and death, and I am silent until thou hast spoken, and when thou hast spoken."

Now what does Christ say? Let us put away, for this time, at least, the words of men, and our own thoughts, and listen to him. I will only ask you to take these two or three sentences of his own words. " The Son of Man is come to seek and to save that which was lost." "This is my body which is broken for you." "This is my blood which is shed for many for the remission of sins." "God so loved the world that he gave his only-begotten Son, that whosoever believeth in him, should not perish, but have everlasting life." "I am the good shepherd; the good shepherd giveth his life for the sheep." This is simply letting him tell his own story. It is not much to allow him to make his own representation of his works, and picture it, if he will. "I am the good shepherd; the good shepherd giveth his life." He does not hint that this is to set the sheep an example or to stir up in them a new love for the shepherd. What they required was to be saved from the wolves. Nothing could be plainer than this presentation of his work. We see the sheep and the wolves, and the Christ. "The good shepherd giveth his life for the sheep."

Now, dear friends, that is the atonement. It is a brief statement, but it is wonderfully clear and satisfying. I ought to say to you candidly that the deepest thought which I ever have upon the atonement comes from such simple sentences as I have now read to you. More and more do I find content in the plain words of Christ himself and the men whom he instructed. The matter is a vital one to me, for my own sake and as your minister. I rejoice to rest my faith, and build my preaching on the truth which Christ taught concerning himself.

The sheep, the wolves, the Christ between — I can understand that as a fact. We may go on a little further, still keeping in the light of the holy Scriptures. When Christ came into the world there were two principles at work. The one was that principle which makes the men who do good blessed. God himself, supremely good, is supremely blessed, and all goodness tends to happiness. Then you find a principle of evil in the world, coming out in lameness and blindness and death, and continually producing unhappiness. On the one side goodness tends to all which we mean by life; and on the other side wickedness tends to all which we mean by death. These two laws prevail; and we find in the Scriptures, as we find in our daily papers and daily walks, that the current thought of the world is away from God; that the ruling passion of men is selfishness and not godliness, and we know that the result can only be unhappiness. With these two forces at work, Christ comes into the world. You will mark that this which I have now described is not a statute, but a necessary relation of cause and effect. It is not God saying, "I command this, that every good man shall be happy, and that every bad man shall be unhappy," giving a law which he may easily reverse. It is not a commandment. It is simply a fact, which is as necessary as the being of God himself, that goodness shall tend to blessedness and to the elevating and the glorifying of the whole character and heart of man. This comes out of the nature of God, and is not the mere command of God. We make a great mistake sometimes when we think we have to deal simply with a code of statutes, which the one administering the law may at any time modify, or repeal. The statutes are as unrepealable as the nature of God. If they should be repealed, you could no longer be certain that God is good, or that he is blessed. I put this down as an everlasting and inevitable truth, that out of goodness comes blessedness, and all which we mean by life.

Into these facts God came with his Spirit and his own nature. With these two principles working among men, God came down and was incarnate in our humanity. He saw men going through their wickedness into their despair. He threw himself in their path. He let this pain and suffering and wrong assail him. He was not made guilty, or he would have been a sufferer merely, and not a deliverer, standing with all the power of his divinity. But, standing with the sympathy of his pure humanity, he let this sorrow, this pain, the malice of sin, fall upon him and overpower him. In doing that he brought in not a new law, but a new working of the law of God. The old principle remained, "The wages of sin is death," and unto this he bowed; but he asserted this new principle: "The free gift of God is eternal life through Jesus Christ our Lord." So that those who had done wrong and to whom sorrow was the inevitable destiny, could be brought out of that course, because the sorrow had fallen upon him. He was not punished, nor compelled, but he took upon himself that which the very nature of things made necessary; the pain which belongs with sin. Christ does this that he may save men. These are the facts. If I were to frame an explanation of them, I would call it the "parental theory." It is God being the Father. If you are a good father, you always insist upon it that only goodness shall have its reward. You tell your child, if you are a Christian mother, from the first time he can understand you, that righteousness tends to happiness, and unrighteousness away from happiness; and you hold your child, by all the force which is in you, to the doing of that which is right. Yet, rather than that your child should suffer for his misdeeds, you would do anything to lead him back and save him. You insist upon it that he must do right. There is not a day in the year when you would not suffer to have him do right, and every day you are giving yourself to this intent. I call it the "mother theory," the "father theory." I write it in with the Lord's prayer: "Our Father who art in heaven; forgive us. Thy kingdom come. Thy will be done on earth" — on this part of the earth where I stand.

I have said all that I wish to say. I should be glad to end here; yet I know the questions which come to your mind. Men say, "If God is love, why is it not enough for a man to turn from the wrong to the right?" It is enough. That is what I have been saying all these years. That is what has been said ever since Christ came into the world. It is enough, if a man turns from the wrong to the right. But what is the right? Right is obedience. There is no turning to the right until you turn to God; and there is no reception there until it is God in mercy to whom you turn; and God in mercy is God in Christ. If you will consistently carry out the turning from the wrong to the right, you will find yourself turning to the grace of God which is in Jesus Christ, his Son. But why is Christ necessary? Why cannot God forgive us just as well without a Saviour? Why cannot we go to God without any thought of Christ? In reply, I say three things: First, we do not have to go to God without Christ. There is no need of it. Why should we seek him by a long path, as if he were afar off, when we can go to him here? Hear Christ's word again: "No man cometh unto the Father but by me." Secondly, it is necessary that God should make an expression of his character, of his nature; and that he should let it work itself out as against all unrighteousness and evil, lest we should feel that sin is such a trifling matter that, whenever we choose to make new resolves everything will be changed in our relation to God.

The third and last thing, which will be to you, as it is to me, the most imperative, is this : God himself appoints the way. He calls us to himself by Christ. Would he have given his Son to the cross if it had not been necessary? You and I may not know why; God knew. Do you say that God is love, and therefore we do not need a Saviour? God loved Christ quite as much as he did men, and he gave him for us and he calls us to him. It is God's way: let us be content, grateful and obedient.

There may come another question : Why is it necessary for us to do anything? Why may we not float upon this tide of God's love into Paradise? I give again three answers : First, we do not need to do this. We can have divine help, we can come to Christ; we can, therefore we should. Secondly, we are free. Character must be made up by our own hands; we have gone away from God of our own will; we must come back to God of our own will. There is no obedience but willing obedience. The third and last reason is this: Christ calls us to believe. " Whosoever believeth," he said. If any man believeth, he shall be saved. When the Holy Spirit comes, following the work of Christ with his divine efficiency, it is not to foster our strength ; to make us feel how good we are ; it is to glorify Christ: to take of the things of Christ and show them unto us, that we may be saved by him.

There are these two things which the text this morning teaches us. One is, that Christ has given himself for our sins. Let us believe that fact; believe it is a fact, and rest in it and love it. Christ says that he has given himself for us, and that there is no need that we should die in our sins. The other teaching is this: that we are to live through him; we are to take his will and do it; to go steadily on in obedience to God who teaches and calls us through Jesus Christ his Son.

That is a beautiful little incident which Doctor Livingstone records concerning his mother. He heard of her death when he was away. He hastened home, and found that death had come to her suddenly. An hour and a half before they thought she was going, her daughter Agnes, sitting by her bedside, said to her, " The Saviour has come for you, mother. You can lippen yourself to him?" Of course she said " Yes;" it was David Livingstone's mother. You know them by their fruits. I think there would be more David Livingstones if there were more such women. She had the natural mother feeling, and had said she would like to have one of her laddies lay her head in the grave; but if none was there, she wished William Logan would do it. David came home in time for that filial office. But there was the simple faith of mother, and daughter, and son, expressed in that Scotch phrase, "You can lippen yourself to him, mother?" You can trust him; you can hold to him, and can rest in his promise as you go your new way.

So I come away from men; and first of all, I come away from myself — out of this poor, inconstant will and way of mine; out of it all to him; not to what he did merely, but to him. There is one Saviour, and that is the Christ himself. Oh, friends, let us "lippen" to Him.

XII.

WE SHALL BE LIKE HIM.

SCRIPTURE LESSON: *Romans* viii: 14–39.

TEXT: Beloved, now are we the sons of God; and it doth not yet appear what we shall be; but we know that when he shall appear, we shall be like him; for we shall see him as he is. *John* iii: 2.

IT doth not yet appear what we shall be." We know as little as this disciple when he wrote these words. He knows more; and many who have gone from our side have gained that great access of knowledge, for they have seen the Lord. But to us it remains true that "it doth not yet appear what we shall be." Hence we gather up with eagerness every hint of the holy Scriptures touching this which is certainly before us, this land upon whose confines we are standing, and into which so many are entering day by day, if we may form to ourselves any conception of that which is coming to us and has come to them. In all the Scriptures there is perhaps no teaching clearer regarding our future life, more level to our comprehension, commending itself more heartily to our thought, than this: in that world which is above us and beyond us, that world of light and love towards which we are looking, the supreme delight, the highest glory, will be this: "We shall be like him, for we shall see him as he is."

But "it doth not yet appear" *where* we shall be in that vast world; nor with what body we shall stand; nor what employment we shall have where still and forever it will be "more blessed to give than to receive"; nor to what glory, what heights of advancement, we shall rise through the eternal training of God, in the endless years. All this "doth not yet appear." It is concealed from our eyes, because it is not possible that it should be written in words. Words cannot describe a sunrise, or a symphony. Words cannot tell what home is, what love is, what life is. If there were words formed, if there were pictures drawn, to make it clear to us what this must be, we should not be able to comprehend the revelation until it had become a part of our own experience. There are certain things which a man can never know until he feels them; until his life enters into them, and is taken up by them. Michael Angelo drawing figures upon the wall and upon the floor, cannot understand what he shall be in that grand career opening before him. David, keeping his flocks, has small notion of the royalty which shall be his; and as he plays his tuneful reeds, he cannot conceive of himself as leading the worship of the saints on earth, perhaps in heaven. We have to enter into these lives and find what love is by loving; what home is by having a home; what life is by living. It is only in this way that we can rise into the conception of that to which we are coming.

This limitation of our powers is for our help. If we could see the glory that is to come, we might be weary of to-day; it might seem harder to do that which we must do — to dig in the ground, to build houses, to handle our gold, to write our books, to give our instruction, to transact our business. This might become intolerable to us; our eyes might not be able to see the implements of our common industry if from the upper world the glory should smite us on the face. We are kept waiting in promise and in hope. It is made certain to us that we are going hence; we are assured that it shall be well for those who depart hence to be with Christ; but what we shall be, in what form of glory we shall spend our eternity, "it doth not yet appear." Yet it is a marked excellence of religion that it turns our thoughts forward.

The Bible, sometimes criticized because it does not deal more thoroughly with the past, with which we have nothing to do, deals thoroughly with the present and the future with which we have everything to do. However much the multitude of books may surpass it in the history of that which has been, it stands solitary in this preëminence, that it tells us of that which is to be; and that which is our present duty and our hope is the practical truth which beyond everything else it becomes us to know. I claim this for the Bible, that it is the most practical of books; and I claim this for religion, that it concerns that to which our interests are most utterly committed; not the past, into which we cannot return, but the future, into which we are sure to enter.

As we read these words of the apostle this morning, we mark a limitation in them. They are set into this present time. "Beloved, *now*," says the apostle; not yesterday, not in the primeval ages; I am speaking to you of that which is now. In this fact of the present stands that which is the promise of all which is to be. "Beloved, now are we the sons of God"—find out, if you can, what you were a myriad years ago; — "*now* are we the sons of God." From this present fact comes this future glory. Because we are now the sons of God, we shall be like him presently, "for we shall see him as he is."

Take, then, this fact first: we are now the sons of God. The good men who have given us our revised version of the New Testament have changed in two respects these words, and for the better. They teach us to read: "Beloved, now are we children of God." They strike out the article which limits it. It is no longer "the sons," but "children." We are children of God by virtue of our nature; we are born of God. We are spirit as God is spirit. We are born again by the Spirit of God, regenerated by him, so that we partake of the divine nature. We receive from God that affection which a father gives his sons, and we return to him that affection which children give their father. We receive that protection, that instruction, that guidance which a father gives his children. We return that obedience, that trust, that submission, which children render to their father. We have our home with him here, and our heaven is to be with God in that which is described by our Lord as our Father's house.

If we take that more restricted use of this term in which it is applied to our Lord himself, the Son of God and the Son of Man, who is the "only begotten Son" of the Father, we find still, in the most wonderful way, the assertion of this fellowship with him. Thus, Jesus himself said, speaking to men: "My Father and your Father." His greatest apostle said that he was "the first-born among many brethern:" the eldest son. In the epistle to the Hebrews it is written that he is not ashamed to call us brethren. When we find these terms applied on the one hand to God as the Father, and on the other to us as his children, we are not to think of them in some loose application, as if they went beyond the fact. The truth is, they do not equal the fact. The words are not large enough. God is our Father in the largest way, and all which we know of fatherhood here is but the likeness to his. The image of fatherhood is in our house; the reality of fatherhood is in God. We imitate fatherhood which has its reality with God. We call ourselves children of our father and mother; the reality is when we are the children of God. The literal is the eternal; the divine is the real; the true fatherhood is in God; the true childhood is the childhood of men to God.

We are not surprised at the use of this name, father, as we feel how tenderly the word reaches us in our lives here; how it comprehends our infancy and blesses us all our days; that we never can become separated from it, and that no man ever gets so old or strong that he does not need his father's counsel and his mother's love; and that the tenderest thoughts, which we keep till the last, are the thoughts of our childhood in the father's house, by our mother's side. And when we are taught to elevate all which is filial and sacred into our thoughts of God, we should be able to rise in faith, and see that this which we know is but the beginning of that which is forever. When one of the missionaries in India was translating this epistle by the aid of a Hindoo youth, he found the young man unwilling to write this sentence. He had written an avowal of God's love, and of the grace which God has shown to men; but when he was told to write, "now are we the sons of God," he wanted to write instead of that, "now we are permitted to kiss his feet."

From this comes, secondly, that revelation of glory which the apostle here brings to our attention. We shall be like God, and therefore like Christ, the Son of God, who is the image of the Father. We are already like him in nature; we shall be like him in character, and in glory. The apostle teaches us that "beholding as in a glass the glory of the Lord, we are changed into the same image from glory to glory." We shall be like him in taste, enjoying what he enjoys, turning away from that which he dislikes. We shall be like him in life and work, finding in his purposes our own law and life, and delighting to do his bidding and to share his work as he is striving to bless men in all places and through all the years. We shall be like God; we shall not be God; we shall not be equal to God; we shall be *like* him; our righteousness shall resemble his; our glory, our spirit, our taste, our occupation shall resemble his.

This is to come, again, because "we shall see him as he is." The very place where we shall see him is favorable to this resemblance of our heart and life to his. Taken away from all that hinders us here, we shall have all the favorable conditions which shall tend to make us like him; all incitements to evil shall be removed; there will be no inclination to selfishness, or earthiness; we shall be broken from the bondage of the flesh, and our very body itself shall be spiritual like the Lord's. We shall stand with a renewed heart where the Holy Spirit shall find us, and the light shall shine through the uncurtained windows of the soul and illuminate our body and our spirit. This putting our weakness away from us and receiving within us the divine strength shall carry us on to the fulfilment of that word, and we shall be like the Lord. We shall be like him because we shall see him. Our Lord's face we shall behold; the tones of his voice we shall hear; we shall keep company with him; in his presence we shall be incited to righteousness. In the presence and power of his will we shall choose to will like him and be holy. Then shall the Lord's Prayer be uttered in the deep sincerity with which we are taught it: "Thy will be done, by me, be done here, in heaven, to-day, as it has been done in heaven by the saints in the past." We shall behold the face of Christ in the light which the Spirit of God shall throw upon it. Then shall his promise be carried further: "The Holy Spirit shall glorify me." He shall hold up in the clear light of heaven the deeds of Christ. "He shall testify of me;" then shall the mystery of the incarnation become plainer, and those deep and weighty truths of redemption become clearer; then shall we be moved to holy living by the sight of that which he has done for us, when it is no longer one afar off, and never seen, whom we are loving, but one whom we see face to face, and of whose love we are continually reminded by the continual manifesting of the same affection. The sight of God — is there anything in all the visions of the future which can surpass this in potency? Is there anything in the future to which we look forward, which is more glorious than to see him as he is? I call to mind those simple words of Laura Bridgman, written in anticipation of that which was before her: " By the finger of God my eyes and ears shall be opened. The string of my tongue shall be loosed. With sweeter joys in heaven I shall hear and speak and see." She has not seen a human face since she was a little child. For fifty years not once has she looked upon a friend. And I said, it is almost worth while to be blind, if the first face which one shall see is the face of Christ. Would you not like to be near that woman when, for the first time, she sees a friendly face and that face is Christ's? It is for us, too. Out of this world we shall rise; out of its darkness into that light; out of its sinfulness into that righteousness; and our eyes blurred with the dust, and dazzled with the glitter, and dimmed with the tears of this world, shall behold the face of God. And we shall be like him when we shall see him as he is.

You will mark, again, that these words have in

them a twofold limitation. It should be frankly confessed, that great as they are, and vast in their expansion, they do restrict the glories of heaven. They limit those who are to enter heaven. The sons of God, the children of God, are to have this delight. They limit again the blessedness of heaven. It consists not in being there, but in being like God. To this twofold limitation we must attend; first, that all who are in heaven are children of God; and, secondly, that the delight of heaven is in being like God. If one, then, is not a child of God, manifestly he is not prepared for this blessedness; and if a man cannot find happiness in being like God, then manifestly he must find that this happines is not for him. And this limitation runs through the Scriptures. Heaven is never spoken of as a broad plain, but as a city — a walled city, a city with its gates and with a path leading to it. Its walls are jewelled, but they are still walls. Every gate is a pearl, but still it is a gate. The door is open, but still it is a door. The path can be trodden, but still it is a path. One comes over the path through the door, into the city; and standing there the child of God, able to enjoy what God enjoys, he has found heaven.

If there be any profit in it, it is very easy to enlarge this. Let us be liberal to-day. The number of those who shall enjoy heaven can be increased by lessening the quality of the happiness, so that more people shall be capable of enjoying it. We can enlarge our college on this plan. Simply degrade it to a grammar school, bring in the studies which are pursued in the lowest schools, and we can multiply our students indefinitely. We can enlarge the number of musicians in the same way. Simply make music include beating a drum, or ringing a bell, and we have increased the number of musical artists. Make science include paving the street with stones, and we can all be scientific men.

What enlargement we can readily make! Yet we say it is better that these professions and institutions should maintain their high standing, and that men should be trained to enter them and enjoy their advantages. That is, instead of degrading the college to a primary school, we may offer to every one who wishes it the opportunity to enter college and pursue liberal studies.

We hold that it is better that music retain its nobility, and that we be trained to appreciate that which is highest and, according to the measure of our ability, really enlarge the melody and harmony of the world. Is it not better that heaven should remain just what it is, and that we should be prepared to enjoy it as it is, than that we should remain as we are and heaven be brought down to us? As it is to-day, no man enters God's heaven who does not love God. Bring down heaven so that everybody is in it, and you have made a place abounding in selfishness. It is this world over again. It is not worth while for a man to take the trouble to die. As well stay here, if heaven is simply an extension of this world, and men there are loving or not loving God, as it may happen; and one trusts him and another does not, and one is kind and another is not, and one worships and another does not. If it is simply the confusion and misrule of this world continued, pray, what have we gained by going to heaven? Is it not rational that we should desire to stay where we are? We may change our idea of heaven. We may broaden the common conception of it. We may make it receive and retain all classes and conditions of men. We can write heaven where we will. But the Bible method is the true one. Let God's heaven remain. Take not a jewel from the walls, not a pearl from the gates; let nothing which defileth pass the threshold; let no earthiness or selfishness enter in; let there be no man there who does not love God and the Saviour, Christ the Lord. Let heaven stand; then train men up for it, teach men to enjoy it, cultivate their taste for it, make them God's children, deliver them from themselves, that they may be worthy of heaven, and thus prepare them for God's heaven. It is nobler and kinder than to degrade heaven into the dust of this world.

The poor boy in the streets of London, watching the royal procession, moved by the glitter of the pageant, says, " This is fine; some day I shall ride in the royal carriage, I shall have the guards about me; I shall be sovereign of England. I am good; I want to be king of England; the queen is kind; she will appoint me king." You tell him that he cannot be king of England because he is not in the royal family. It is the queen's eldest son who is to be king. But what if there were two kings, as in Siam; what if there were a thousand kings, as among the African tribes? Still, one must have royalty to come to the regal estate.

It is possible to-day for a man to become God's child; then he has the benefits and blessings of God's children. You say that God calls everybody his child and loves everybody. It is true; more true than you think. But the true child loves as well as receives love. Childhood needs the answering heart of man if it is to have the child's blessing. We can be God's children in the high and true sense. It is written, "As many as received him, to them gave he the right to become children of God." Would you rather that were written in this way: "He gave a selfish man the right to enjoy heaven?" It is better to change the man and let the heaven remain. Or take our Lord's assurance that we must be — that is, we may be — "born of the Spirit of God." To be born of God is to be his child and his heir. Or recall these words, "The Son of Man is come to seek and to save that which was lost." Or these, "I give unto my sheep eternal life, and they shall never perish, neither shall any man pluck them out of my hand." The whole burden of the Gospel is this: "There is a glorious heaven, full of all delight, of supreme and everlasting blessedness; and I am here to prepare you to enter it." Shall we cry, "Lord, bring heaven down to us?" No; he will bring us up to heaven. "Lord, change heaven so that a selfish man can enjoy it?" No; he will change the selfish man so that he can enjoy the heaven which is. "Lord, change heaven so that a man can enjoy it who never loved the Lord and Saviour?" No; he will let heaven stay precisely as it is, and change us so that we shall love and trust and serve the Lord of heaven.

This is the method of the Gospel. It is a grand, broad hope; it is the larger hope; it leaves heaven on the heights and with its glories unharmed; it offers to every child of man, the world over, the opportunity of entering into it. It withholds no man; it makes it too difficult for no man. It does not stretch out the walls of heaven until they enclose this earth with all its earthiness: it lets the walls remain. It does not take away the door, as Samson carried the gates of Gaza, but it opens the door, and leaves it standing open. It does not drive us in, or force heaven around us, as the waters rising make an island of a man's house, but it stands at the open door of God's heaven and cries, "Whosoever will — without money and without price —

whosoever will, wherever he is, let him come. Every joy of heaven is his, all the wealth of heaven is his; the summons is free to everlasting glory. Behold, I have set before you an open door into God's enduring grace." Surely we are gainers by this method. Let heaven stand. It is for all men, in the Father's love for all men. The Father calls all men; Christ gave himself for all men; "the Spirit and the Bride say come." The wealth of God and the pure joys of his heaven are offered to us for the taking. Let us promptly and gratefully accept the grace of God, that we may enjoy the riches of his love in his heaven.

Let us mark the breadth of this, and feel, first, that heaven is very great and good, and then, that it is offered to every one of us. Every man is asked to become the child of God; every man who will can be the child of God. "Ye will not come to me," Jesus said. It may be that we shall fail of heaven. But we shall not fail of God's heaven because there is a door, for the door is open; nor because we are not called, nor because we cannot come. If we fail of God's heaven it is because we will not be the children of God.

Perhaps we shall get a clearer idea if we remember that this heaven which is above us is Christ's heaven. He has made it, he will enjoy it. It is such a heaven as is pleasant to him. If, now, we are to enjoy the same heaven, then we must be like him, and able to enjoy what Christ enjoys.

Whenever we come it must be with a preparation to enjoy the things of Christ, There are visions of the future which many are cherishing, that somewhere, beyond this world, down the ages, all men will enter into the kingdom of heaven. If it is so, they must come in the one way. A million years hence heaven will be as it is to-day. No man can ever enjoy heaven until he is qualified to enjoy what Christ enjoys. No man can ever enter heaven, ages and ages hence, but through that which Christ has done. No man will ever be fitted to enjoy Christ's heaven until the Spirit of God has made him a child of God. Time has nothing to do with that. There is no change of method. If we ever find our way into the city, it will be through that open door, and the door will be there forever and forever.

If this be true, should we not find the beginning of heaven here, by choosing here what Christ likes? If we can enjoy the things of Christ now, then we shall have the enjoyment of his presence here. We can have the sight of his face which shall fill us with joy. It was a pleasant remark of the woman through whose guidance so many are "stepping heavenward," when speaking of her scholars and their trivial ways and words, she exclaimed, "Oh, but this *is* such a nice world, and the girls do not know it!" Yes, this is a good world, and we do not know how good it is. But the greatest joy which comes to men in this life is the joy of being like Christ; having his will, his character, his spirit, his confidence in the Father, his anticipation of the glory to come. These we can have here to-day. He said many things touching heaven. Sometimes a man goes out at the dawn, and looking up at the star which heralds the day, admires its beauty, and there comes a voice out of the excellent glory: "To that man, who, rising early, comes forth to serve me through the day, I will give the morning star." He looks up to the sky which is above him, and thinks of the temple of God with its roof glittering with the light which is celestial and eternal; and he wonders what shall hold up the everlasting beauty! "That man who comes forth to his work loving me and doing my will from day to day, I will make him a pillar in the temple of my God." Who shall rule there, and what shall be the spirit and the law of heaven, where the throne of God and of the Lamb is set? "That man who, kneeling here, devotes his life to me in this world, makes himself pure of heart and does the deeds which are pleasing in my sight, I will grant to him to sit with me in my throne."

But oh, beloved, to own the morning star, to be a pillar in the temple, to sit upon the throne, cannot allure and comfort us and draw our thought and life upward and onward as does this simple word which we have read to-day. Here in this weakness and this sin; here with this poor vision and these faltering hopes; here with these disappointments and defeats, the great comfort which comes to a man is that there is a day when he shall be like Him. With glad voice he cries, " I shall be like Him, for I shall see Him ; I shall see Him as he is."

XIII.

THE UNCHANGING CHRIST.

SCRIPTURE LESSON : *Hebrews*, i.
TEXT : Jesus Christ the same yesterday, and to-day, and forever. *Hebrews* xiii: 8.

JESUS CHRIST is the same yesterday and to-day, yea, and forever." It is in this way that the new version teaches us to read the sentence. There is here the assertion of two facts: first, that our Lord has eternal life; his eternal yesterday, his endless years; and secondly, that through this eternity he has been, and ever more shall be, the same.

We are accustomed to make a threefold division of Christ's life, though not always in these words. We think of the part preceding his entrance into the world, then of the time which he spent among us; and then of the years in which he now is living. It is not difficult for us to feel — indeed, it is our common thought — that during the long periods before and since his incarnation, our Lord is the same. We regard his life here, perhaps, as a break in his career, a change in his condition, while the parts before it and after it hold him in the sameness of his character.

Let us look, for a moment, at the fact that Christ is the same yesterday and forever. We do not need to dwell upon it. I remind you simply of these sayings of Scripture regarding him. First, "In the beginning was the Word, and the Word was with God, and the Word was God." " The Word became flesh, and dwelt among us." Then, upon the other hand, for the future, " Unto the Son he saith, Thy throne, O God, is forever and ever." Or take this saying of our Lord's, when, looking forward, he prayed to the Father : " Glorify thou me with thine own self with the glory which I had with thee before the world was ;" thus bringing his past into his future and asking for the endless ages only that which in the unbegotten eternity he had enjoyed.

It is not upon this that I wish to dwell, but rather upon this fact : that our Lord, during the brief interval between the "yesterday" and the to-morrow, the time which is here called the "to-day," was the same as during these years before and after that brief period. We are surprised, perhaps, that this should be so. Our common thought is of a change — the greatest change that could be made; a change which it beggars language to describe. Is it not written of him — and to find it we do not need to turn beyond the simple record of his own life — that the word which was in the beginning became flesh? Surely no change could be greater than that. He was worshipped by the angels, and yet he was made a little lower than the angels. He was rich, yet for our sake he became poor. Take that sentence of St. Paul's in which the two facts are asserted, that he was "in the form of God," " but emptied himself, taking the form of a servant; and being found in fashion as a man, he humbled himself, becoming obedient even unto death, yea, the death of the cross." Then for the future : " Wherefore also God highly exalted him, and gave unto him the name which is above every name." Surely as we read from one passage to another and mark these transitions, it is difficult to believe that he is the same in this to-day that he was in the yesterday.

Or, if we should take the outward circumstances as they are presented to us, and mark the change, we have the coming from heaven to earth; the exchange of a throne for a manger; the worship of angels for the rejection of men; the blessedness of his eternity for the wounding, the smiting, the rejection, which here were visited upon him. It is a giving up of life for death upon the cross. It is coming from that endless brightness into the gloom of the sepulchre. Is there any change conceivable greater than this? What, then, means this word of the Scripture which is written in among these marvellous transitions, that Jesus

Christ to-day, in this world, in all its wretchedness, and upon its cross, is the same that he is enthroned in heaven, in the endless years which are before and after us?

We are familiar with the fact that a man's outward condition may change without any change in the man. It is not so common as it ought to be; yet it is not so rare that we do not often recognize it. We mark one coming from his boyhood into his manhood, taking on the responsibilities of life, doing its work, filling its offices, administering its trust, gathering its treasures, and then passing into a serene old age which bears him on to his immortality; but through all these changes remaining still the same, keeping the simplicity of his boyhood, retaining his quick and vigorous conscience, never suffering to be obliterated the distinction between right and wrong which he learned at his mother's side; never forgetting the simple maxims of morality which were taught him in the Sabbath-school, fashioning all his life by the unchanging rules of right, keeping the tenderness and sweetness of his affection. We are familiar with a change which is not the change of the man, even within a single day, as when a strong man rises in the morning, makes his prayer before God, plays with his children, goes out into the stress of life, spends the day upon the exchange, in the court room, in the workshop, comes home at night, to the seclusion of his own fireside, to lay off all the harness of the day and all the cares of life; and yet from first to last is the same man, moved by the same spirit, as really living for God at noonday as at midnight; as really living for his children when they are out of his mind and he is only working for them, as when he holds them upon his knee or joins in their childish sports. We say of him, from the morning when he prayed, through the day in which he toiled, in the evening when he rested, that he is the same man. Open his heart: no change has passed upon it; his purposes have suffered no alteration, his affections have not been modified. From morning to noon, and noon to midnight, he is still the same.

Now these changes which have come upon Christ's life are changes of condition which do not necessarily involve a change of character. To come from heaven to earth, from the throne to the cross, does not show any change in him. Indeed, it is an attribute of a great nature to be able to come from the throne to the manger, and to be the same in the manger that it was upon the throne. The man who is able in all places to be the same, is the oak and not the orchid; is the man of God and not the man of this world; and is living by an unchanging law. It is saying a great deal, but it is not saying too much, nor stepping beyond the true conception of his character, to say that in his humiliation there was nothing to change Christ; that, whether he was worshipped by angels, or mocked by men; whether he was receiving gifts or giving himself, he was the same. It is the royalty of manhood to be independent of conditions; it is an essential part of the divinity of Christ.

Yet we stand in wonder and admiration before the changes in Christ's life. I know of nothing to which they can be closely compared. I have thought of a man at home; a father, great and rich, whose house is furnished with all luxuries, whose children live in his love. From this father, out of this home, a son wanders away; goes down into the "far country;" wastes his substance, forgets his home. Then the father, leaving his house, goes after his son. He gives up his business for the search; spends his money and his time that he may reclaim his son; suffers for him; gives himself in sacrifice; at last finds him and brings him home. It is the father who has done this. He is the same man in the far country that he was in his home; the same man in his seeking and saving that he was in the repose of his own dwelling. It is because of a love which is equal to the search, that he goes down to bring back his wandering, his lost son. And I said, when God comes down out of heaven and is made flesh, he has not become some one else; he is the same God, striving to bring us back to himself by his unchanging love. Hence, we read this sentence of the Scripture: that the Lamb of God who was given for us in sacrifice was "slain from the foundation of the world." We read again in the words of the apostle that God hath "saved us, and called us with a holy calling; not according to our works, but according to his own purpose and grace, which was given us in Christ Jesus before times eternal, but hath now been manifested by the appearing of our Saviour Christ Jesus."

If, now, we examine the life of our Lord as it is lived before us here in the world, we shall see that it is not held within the common limits, but is connected with a life which is not bounded by time, nor confined by events.

From first to last he is living as one whose years here are but a part of a life which began long before, and will continue after he has gone hence. His entrance upon life is not of this world. The Holy Ghost descends; the power of the Highest overshadows the Virgin; and the holy thing which is born of her, is called the Son of God. He bears two names. He is called "Jesus, for it is he that shall save his people from their sins." He is called by the angel "Immanuel, God with us." Of the years which follow we know almost nothing. Thirty years out of the thirty-three lie in obscurity. There is not a legend to be trusted. Not an incident is known except the interview of a boy twelve years old with the doctors in the temple. The years lie in their mystery. They are lost in the brilliancy of the ages before and after them.

As he moves through life he is clearly in connection with the past. He does not say, " I am here," but "I came;" "I was sent;" "God loved the world and gave his Son." He is continually in contact with the unseen. The heavens part, and the Holy Ghost descends in bodily form like a dove and abides upon him. He goes among the cliffs of Hermon, and his face becomes dazzling and his garments white, " so as no fuller on earth can white them." Angels herald his coming, succor him in his temptation, minister to him in the garden, watch his sepulchre, attend him on the mount of his ascension. He had but to lift his pierced hand and more than twelve legions of angels who were so near that he could touch them would have rescued him from his captors. He spends nights upon the mountains in communion with his father. He hears voices which no man can interpret; some say it thunders; others that an angel spake to him. He talks with God as a man with his father. He declares that his kingdom is not of this world. Standing here, in all his humility, he says, "Ye shall see the heaven opened, and the angels of God ascending and descending upon the Son of Man." Thus he lives, not as belonging in Nazareth or Bethlehem, in Jerusalem or Samaria, but as one whose home is above. His Father's house is beyond the world. He is tarrying here with his glory upon him, and it comes even to his death, of which he says, " Now is the Son of Man glorified."

He lived three and thirty years in Palestine: but there is not a spot in the land which can be connected with his presence, save only Jacob's well at Samaria, where in his weariness he rested. He reads his biography from Moses and the prophets. In the time of his transfiguration the Lawgiver and the Prophet come and talk with him of that which was well known in heaven, and would be celebrated here for centuries. Surely he lives in contact with the past and with the years to come; in communion and fellowship with the unseen.

His teachings were of the same character. Even the people said that he taught like no other teacher they had known. There was a strange authority about his words. The officers who were sent to bring him to the Sanhedrim, came back without him, and said, "Never man so spake." He spoke upon themes of the most vital interest: God, duty, immortality, the grace of God, the gift of God, the judgment and the life to come. Men sometimes had talked of these things, but no one had ever spoken clearly until he declared the truth. He taught with authority which intelligence and honesty could not resist. His words remain today, still strong and fresh. The world has no system of ethics like the Sermon on the Mount. The world has not yet risen to the plane of the morality which he taught, and enforced, and illustrated with the wisdom which was his in the eternal yesterday.

If we pass to his works it is quite the same. No one ever worked like him. Others had wrought miracles by the power of God; he wrought miracles by his own power. His miracles had long before been named. They were in the record of the past. You find scarcely anything said of them in the Gospel which was not written in the prophets. You have but to fix names and dates to what the prophets said, and you find recorded in the Old Scriptures the works which are the miracles of the New. You can read the Gospel almost as well in Isaiah as in John. There was no reason why his life should not be described centuries before he came into the world, for he was living, with his purposes formed, from the beginning. Our plans may come to nothing. With God to plan is to do. God's intention is God's action. God's purpose is as certain as its accomplishment will be. God's to-morrow is as fixed as his yesterday. Hence Christ had but to live out the endless purpose which he had with the Father, and his life would pass into this earthly stage and go on into its glory. Indeed, we might say that the very works which such an one must do if he comes here, are these works which he did. It is a wonderful evidence of the truth of the miracles, that no one else has done works like them. It is sometimes said that these miracles cannot be true, because they are not common; we ought to see other persons doing the same thing. But their singularity is a witness to their reality. If they were common, they would not be miracles. If others did them, the Christ would not be content with them. It is because no one else ever did them, and no one else ever will do them; it is because in all human might there is nothing like the miracles of Christ, that his miracles are true and the witness to his divinity, to his yesterday, and his to-morrow. For we may be sure that if the Word becomes flesh and dwells among men, it will not be content with the duties of the common life, the ordinary work, the customary usefulness of men. He will not content himself in wandering over the hills about Nazareth, and communing with nature, and drawing in its strength and inspiration, and using these in the years of his public ministry. If Christ is here, he will do what no one else has done. The blind will receive their sight, the deaf will hear, the lame will leap, the dead will be raised up, and the poor will have the Gospel preached to them. If there have not been done upon the earth such things as never before and never since were wrought, then the Jew is right and the Christ is yet to come. Christ is not yet to come to redeem the world. The Christ has come; the everlasting yesterday has become to-day.

His death was in keeping with his life. No one ever died as he died. The teachings of Scripture seem to be set aside when they approach his death. "Yea, though I walk through the valley of the shadow of death, I will fear no evil; for thou art with me; thy rod and thy staff they comfort me." How many have lived in the faith of these words? Yet, when he came to his death, forsaken and despised of men, suffering under the darkened heavens, the "rod" was not stretched out for him, and the "staff" did not comfort him. He did not go to his death unwillingly, as one overpowered. He gave his life. "No one taketh it away from me; but I lay it down of myself," he said. No one else ever claimed for his death such power as he claimed. He claimed for his death more than for his life. "And I, if I be lifted up from the earth will draw all men unto myself!" "I lay down my life for the sheep," for "I am the good shepherd." Men must feed upon his broken body, and drink his blood, to have the life which he gives, and his blood is shed "unto the remission of sins." It was not possible that he should be holden of death. Stone, seal, soldiers, Jewish malice and Roman might could be of no avail. When upon the dial plate of heaven the moment of the third day had struck, he came out from the sepulchre. Had all the trees of the garden been soldiers, with their spears close as the rustling leaves, it would have made no difference. When the hour had come, Christ must come. There was the yesterday which nothing in to-day could master. The eternal could not be entombed.

He rose from the dead; he revealed himself to men; he stood among his disciples and reached his hands over them in blessing, and was parted from them, and received up into his glory. Through all his life what claims he made: "Before Abraham was, I am;" "I am the resurrection;" "I am the life;" "I am the way;" "No man cometh unto the Father but by me;" "No man can come to me except the Father draw him." Recall that grandest of all promises which has nothing to exceed it. "I give unto them eternal life;" I give eternity; I give an eternity of life.

I have mentioned certain features of our Lord's life, that we may see how closely his to-day is connected with the eternal yesterday and to-morrow. If we regard the life as a whole, the same unity appears. The endless proportions entered into his being and character. He had the traits of no nation, the limitations of no age. He was the Son of Man, of mankind in its every generation, in its early purpose and endless destiny. He had the wisdom of Him who was from eternity. His power, his holiness and justice, his goodness and truth, were not human attributes, born of the present, belonging to this world. In their perfection was the witness to his eternity. He amazed the doctors at the temple when he was but a boy. He always surprised men. He is still the wonder. His glory was disclosed at times; but the concealment of his glory was a part of his humiliation. His words were his witness; and his silence was in keeping with his words. He displayed his might; but the withholding of his power is as impressive as his miracles. His commandments declared his authority, while his gentleness and compassion and patience marked his control of men, and, like his authority, were not of to-day. He was master when he was servant, and servant when he was master. Among sinful men he was separate from sinners in his holiness. Between men in their affairs he was just, and he declared his enduring justice. Tempted like men, his goodness and truth were his comfort before his Father when he was to die for the sins of the world. This is a divine career. Yesterday and forever meet in to-day. Study his life in its details; examine its majestic proportions; note its revelations and its concealments; mark its spirit and its word and deed; trace it from its opening when the heavens were thronged with angels and the midnight air was filled with their songs, to its close, when the sun was darkened, and angry men denounced him and soldiers cast lots for his raiment, while he died between the malefactors, and on to the hour of his resurrection, when he burst the bands of death and the grave. Continue with him in a quiet, reverent, grateful, loving sympathy: let him breathe upon you; let him open his heart, and tell his hopes to you, and manifest the love which is beyond all men's; walk with him, rest with him, live and love with him;

let his grace fall upon your life and his blessing become your own experience; and it will become clear, more and more clear, that this precious to-day is not his life: nor this with the eternity which is beyond. The past is his. He is the same yesterday, and to-day, and forever. Such a life is not of the earth earthy. It does not bear the superscription of time. It needs a past to account for it, and it cannot pass away. Nothing is simpler in the presence of the Christ than that which the Gospel teaches: The Word was in the beginning; the Word became flesh; the Word shall be forever. He is, and was, and is to come, the Almighty. To him be the glory and the dominion forever and ever.

This is the Saviour who comes to us for our homage and trust; who asks not our chance thought, for he gave us no chance thought; who requires the ruling purpose of our life, the devotion of our thought and work to him, that as he lived for us we may live unto him in an unchanging love, the same in the sanctuary and in the world, the same in this world as in heaven, with our to-day making up our to-morrow.

In the light of this subject, we see, first: The grandeur of this redemption in which we stand. It is no thought of man; it is the great, the endless thought of God. He has given himself for us. He has come to us, carrying out his purpose, this endless purpose of his grace. Let us not think of

God as changing, but as keeping us in his unchanging love.

Secondly, in the persistence of our Lord's purposes, and the constancy of his love, we have great comfort. His ways are long. His plans are not affected by the events which break our years. A thousand years are one day to him. What we name death is a change in our life, not in his intention or promise. We are to keep this in mind, that we may understand him and order our thoughts wisely. One of our greatest mistakes is in attempting to confine his promises within the brief spaces of our life. It is not the highest doctrine, but it is a serviceable principle, the doctrine of waiting. We ask men to suspend their judgment till we have completed the work which they are examining; and not to accuse us of breaking our word till the time has passed in which the word can be kept. Let us be honorable with God, and be still while his work is incomplete.

He brings one into great prosperity, and the man blesses him. He takes away the riches, and the man cries out against God. "For all life is unroofed, and the tempests beat through." Let the man be still, and see what will come afterwards. The plan has not changed. The road which led up the mountain has gone down on the other side. When it has passed through the valley, it will ascend again. Meantime there are green pastures and still waters in the valley, and the man can look up to the hills. Wait now and see what the Lord will do with you. Trust him and obey, and you shall be content.

A child is born into the world, and his cradle is made an altar where parental hearts offer their sacrifice of prayer, and say in their confidence, "It is God's child"; and they name him with the name of God. It is right. The child grows into glad and hopeful youth. He will be a man in whom his parents will more than live again, and the world will be stronger for his coming.

The vision fades. The youth falters, his eye loses its light, his hand its cunning. He has gone. The Lord has taken him. The Lord has changed his place, but has not changed his own design. His plan has advanced, and borne the young man forward with it. In another world, in other employments, he will fulfil his career. Hope has ascended and entered its eternal form. The plan of the Lord for them to whom the surprise and disappointment have come has not changed. He meant it for good when he gave them their delight, and his good thought continues with them, and in his time will bear them on into the world whither their treasure has preceded them. They will be satisfied when they awake in the perfect day. They will be satisfied here even in their sorrow and longing, when they can see the unchanging wisdom, the unalterable love, and the endless purpose of their God.

Again, it is in this unchanging character of God that we have the ground of our hope of eternal life. The original plan of God regards the guilt of men. When he created the world he meant to redeem it: else he would not have created it. When he saw that all things were very good, he saw the cross of Christ. Sinai and Calvary were before him. He saw the tree of life, and the altar of life. The sin of man is not a surprise to him, creating an emergency for which he was not prepared. He made men free, and knew the result in advance. He bestows a love which would last. Man destroys himself, but he does not destroy the love of God. He breaks the commandments, but he does not break the purpose in which the commandments have their place. By his sin man changes himself, changes the world, changes his relation to God, changes his destiny. But the love of God remains. It seeks man in his new estate. It gives itself for him in sacrifice. If the man will turn, will return to God, he will find the love waiting to receive him; nay, running to him with the kiss of welcome and forgiveness. Those are majestic words, rich in comfort and hope, which are written as the Old Testament closes: "I am the Lord, I change not; therefore ye sons of Jacob are not consumed." The Saviour whom we trust is not born of this present time. He is the same yesterday, and forever, and to-day.

Hence we see that there is no need that some men, some saints, some glorified spirit should come between us and God. We can come directly to our Father. There is no one nearer than he, no one more loving. We can bring our confession and our prayer directly to him. But does not the Scripture say, "There is one God, one mediator also between God and man, himself man, Christ Jesus?" But who is the "man Christ Jesus?" It is the eternal word become flesh; so that when I come to him, I come to God. Jesus said, "No one cometh unto the Father but by me;" he also said, "No man can come to me except the Father which sent me draw him." He also said that he could do nothing of himself: "I and the Father are one." If I may recur to my illustration, it seems like this: when the father goes out from his house to seek his wayward son and bring him home, he is a mediator between himself in the house and the son in the country. He is not some one who is neither father nor son. He is the father, only he is the father out of doors. He is the father in sacrifice. It is the unchanging love, working in a new condition. The God who is the mediator is the God incarnate. God in Christ is a mediator between us and God who is not in Christ. God here, teaching, leading, helping, saving, is the mediator between us and God who has sent him into the world; and he that hath seen him hath seen the Father. I do not come to Christ that I may come to God; I come to Christ because God is in Christ. In him I meet the Father. "Who can forgive sins but God alone?" Yet "the Son of man hath power on earth to forgive sins." We cannot have a divided allegiance of gratitude for our salvation. One is the Saviour, even he who is "the same yesterday and to-day and forever."

We see, finally, the reality of the communion of saints. All men can unite in this love of God. Separate as we are by race, by language, by taste, by a thousand things, we can come together in this. Here, around the Lord's table, the yesterday and the to-morrow meet in the to-day. How shall those born centuries ago understand this which is before us to-day in the communion? Yet there is nothing in our life which will be more familiar to the saints of the distant times than this table which is before us. Let Abraham stand with us and learn what this meaneth. But that friend of God would say, "This is the promise which was made to me. Your own records trace from me the descent of the Christ. I was told that in me all the families of the earth should be blessed. I desired to see the day of Christ; and I saw him and was glad." Let Moses come to see here the fulfilment of the sacrifices which he ordained; he who on Hermon met our Lord and talked with him of his decease which he has accomplished at Jerusalem. Let Isaiah come, and unfold his own scroll and read in his own words of this which is here set before us; of him who was "wounded for our transgressions, and bruised for our iniquities." Let David come, with his antique garb, with his strangeness of language and demeanor, to be surprised at many things he would see; surprised at the plainness of our house and the simplicity of our worship; yet needing but a moment to bring him into sympathy with us when his eyes fall upon the table. As we call it the table of the Lord, and with glad hearts gather around it, he would say, "I know what this means; I wrote it long ago. I blessed the Lord and sang, 'Thou preparest a table before me.' 'They shall be abundantly satisfied with the fatness of thy house; and thou shalt make them drink of the river of thy pleasures.'"

But this is the crucifixion of the Messiah; he of whom you sung as a king was given to the cross. "I said that he should be given to the cross. Did I not write of him, 'I am poured out like water, and all my bones are out of joint'. They pierced my hands and my feet." But when he was upon the cross, they mocked him and cried, "He trusteth on God, let him deliver him now, if he desireth him." "I said that they should do so; you may read in the twenty-second Psalm how they that mocked him cried, 'He trusted on the Lord that he would deliver him; let him deliver him, seeing he delighted in him.'" The soldiers divided his garments among them. "I said that they should do so ; 'They part my garments among them, and cast lots upon my vesture.'" Fearful was his suffering upon the cross, and he cried, "I thirst." "I said that he should thirst," David would make answer: "'My strength is dried up like a potsherd; and my tongue cleaveth to my jaws; and thou hast brought me into the dust of death.'" But they gave him vinegar to drink. "I said, 'They gave me also gall for my meat, and in my thirst they gave me vinegar to drink.'" He called upon God, as one forsaken in his dying. "I said that it should be so; that he should cry, 'My God, my God, why hast thou forsaken me? why art thou so far from helping me?'" But he was rescued from the grave. Do not think, David, that he was cast into the sepulchre there to remain forever. "I said that he should not remain in the grave: 'My flesh also shall rest in hope; for thou wilt not leave my soul in hell; neither wilt thou suffer thine Holy One to see corruption. Thou wilt show me the path of life; in thy presence is fulness of joy; at thy right hand there are pleasures for evermore." Let David come. Let all who are able to remember the atoning death of the Messiah, who is the Son of God, join in this sacrament. Of all the goodly fellowship in the household of this ancient church, not one will be more welcome, not one will be more at home, than the saints of the elder time who looked for the Messiah beforehand; and wrote the story of his redemption in promises and songs, whose meaning they little knew, but whose meaning we have come to see.

Brethren, this is forever. We are going on to behold this unchanging Christ in fellowship with the prophets and with the apostles. It is asked if the Lord will wear forever the body of his humiliation. I believe that is the common thought. The catechism encourages us to believe that evermore in heaven we shall see the nail-prints and the thorn-prints and the spear-prints. It may be so; I do not know. We shall know soon. But I have this fancy — it is little more than a fancy — that our Lord will not be forever "mortgaged to our humanity," but bringing all our humanity up to the plane of Jesus of Nazareth, will be incarnate in all his ransomed ones; and that then we shall see more clearly what that word meaneth which teaches us that the church is "the body of Christ."

Certainly we shall see him; whatever form he wears we shall see him and know him. His unchanging love, his gentleness, compassion, forgiveness, these we shall see. The Christ whom we behold to-morrow is the Christ of the eternal yesterday, the Christ of this to-day. "I am the Alpha and the Omega, the first and the last, the beginning and the end." Thou art the same, O thou Christ of God, yesterday, to-day, and forever. Glory be unto thee, O Lord, Saviour of men; "as it was in the beginning, is now, and ever shall be, world without end. Amen."

XIV.

THE WAYSIDE SEED.

SCRIPTURE LESSON : *Matthew* xiii: 1-23.
TEXT : And when he sowed, some seeds fell by the wayside, and the fowls came and devoured them up. *Matthew* xiii: 4.

> What though the seed be cast by the wayside,
> And the birds take it — yet the birds are fed.

NOT in vain had the seed fallen from the sower's hand. It brought him nothing in the harvest; but the fowls were the better for it. He had that comfort, that he had fed those who were not made to sow, or reap, or gather into barns. Two of them might be sold for a farthing; but "your Heavenly Father feedeth them." Then it was not too small a thing for a man to do. Their title to the seed was the same as his. It rested upon finding it; upon the care of Him who had provided enough for man and bird. The breeze bore the grains where the sower would not have cast them. But the breeze was from above, and the sower's toil and treasure were not wasted. It might come to pass that the birds should in some way repay his unintentioned care for them.

Meantime it is no slight honor and privilege to be the hand of the Almighty and to care for his smallest ones, dropping his love, which has taken on the form of seed, where they can find it. The other gentle words of our Lord, of the sparrows which cannot fall without your Father, words full of comfort, with their generous revealing of the Providence which watches over us, easily find our heart, to make us trustful, and patient, glad that we know a God so kind and constant, and a Saviour who could bestow the strength of his care. There is a quiet evangel in the lessons of the birds and of Him who guards and feeds them. It is good to read together all which our Lord said about them. It is good to find in this morning's parable that we may share with God this ministry of life, and be his visible Providence; that a part of his thought and purpose and goodness is revealed by us who have this fellowship with God, and manifest his nature; that his kindness can overflow our hands like

> Rivers, to whose falls
> Melodious birds sing madrigals.

It is happening to us all to repeat this part of our Lord's parable. We are sowing as we go on. Some seed falls by the wayside. We have our purposes, and invest our efforts in them, and look for a return which shall make us richer. Our mind is on the harvest as we scatter the seed.

But just beyond our plan, and aside from our thought, our endeavor falls. There is no harvest, or the ingathering is scant. Still something has been done which was worth the doing. At least the birds have been fed. For example, a man invests his money in a factory, and means to increase his property by the investment. The year ends and he has no more than when the year began. He has no more, but the birds have had more. He has lived, and he has given bread to those who have toiled for him, furnished their homes, taught their children, preserved them for better days.

So in all kinds of business. There may be times when the pecuniary return is very small, even less than nothing, while yet we have lived upon our industry, and others have been supported by the work; saved from hunger and want; kept and brought up to be useful in the world by the wayside seed. Every life has this unintentioned usefulness. If we do our work well, it cannot be but that some one will be the better off. The end which we seek may not be gained, but these incidental benefits will not be wanting. These may be greater in real worth than the things we sought. Just as a river may do more good by overflowing its banks and watering the adjacent meadows than by sending its swift currents into the deep sea. It was in this wayside flowing that the bread cast upon the waters came back after many days; not at the mouth of the Nile, but on the fields over which it had passed incidentally, the bread was found. In the family we may find this side influence; the highest parental hopes may not be realized, but something will come from the home life. In the school, the pupil may not prove an apt scholar in his regular lessons, while yet he is learning other lessons by the way. In our philanthropy we may not see our desire fulfilled, and yet we may be doing good in some different method.

In our efforts for our personal good we may not attain to our ideal and become what we meant, but we may be growing on every side; building up our character, increasing in all manly grace and strength, proving our right to live. It is possible that in all these ways we may secure better results than we sought, albeit they be not the same. Perhaps feeding the birds may be better than filling our barns.

Let us take this comfort as we go on. We have need of encouragement. We lay out our work somewhat in the dark, and plan at a venture. In few lives is the accomplishment like the intention. In most lives it seems less. We come to middle life, and then to old age, with a feeling of discontent. How often we say, how deeply we feel, that life has been a failure. The years of promise have come and gone, and what is there to show for them? What have we done which needed so much time? It will be some solace, and we have a title to it, that we have done many side things;

have touched other lives; have helped to keep the family, the Church, and society; have dropped good words, given money, bestowed sympathy, visited the sick, lent a helping hand, while our main work has been running on without accomplishing all we designed. The birds have been fed, and the birds are our Father's, and the seed was his.

Not all who seem to fail, have failed indeed.

Our lives are intertwined. We dwell together and work in company. No life moves on by itself, complete in its own bounds. Life is not a sluggish canal, but a rapid stream which brings into its current the mountain brooks and the branches which water the meadows, and perhaps becomes itself the branch of a large river. It is a matter of opinion which is the largest river in our land. It would be more difficult to determine which is the most useful stream, or at what point any one is of most service.

It is not easy to measure lives, or the parts of a life. A great life may take its character more from some undesigned influence, than from the effort which has sought to control it. A life may do more by turning the course of another life which it has not meant to affect than it does with design in the steady round of its vocation. If we could all speak, doubtless many would acknowledge this indebtedness to men who did not know that they were helping them. Perhaps some would confess that they have been most influenced by those who have not tried to order their ways for them. What a blessed thing it is that the Lord who knows all we do will reward those who do good when they do not know that they are doing it!

Would it do to leave all things to this incidental working; simply to go our way and be busy, and believe that, wittingly or unwittingly, we are doing all the good which can be required of us? Very much is said of unconscious influence, and said with truth. Shall we, then, simply pursue our daily work, and think that we are helping the world on without any special care or pains of ours?

It might be answered that the world is not content with our unconscious influence and incidental benevolence, but is very sure to demand our attention and to insist on decided and deliberate action. It intrudes itself into our homes, and states its wants with persistent iteration. The birds may be trusted to come to us. If the seed is not on the ground, they will flutter about the granary and even peck at our closed hand. Who shall say it is not their right? Whence comes the instinct of the bird, of the man? Larger barns have less warrant in the Gospel than larger doors for small barns.

The Church is constantly calling for direct

personal service. With a definite work to do she summons us to thoughtful devotion. She asks of all men time and presence and effort. Would it not be as well for the Church to allow men to work by themselves, and to do good incidentally; if not by divine methods, yet by methods of their own; if not in the field, yet along the wayside? I think that the Church will consent to this as soon as men in their usual occupations will agree to it; when they will be satisfied with the wayside results; when they will build factories to support the workmen, and send out ships for the good of the sailors, and pursue their business in the interest of their clerks, and keep up their houses that the servants may have homes, and be satisfied though they get no other return for their investments; when they will care nothing for the harvest, so that the birds are fed; when it is a general benevolence and not a desire for a fair personal advantage which is the mainspring of their exertion; and good done is held equivalent to gain secured; then, I think, the Church will be ready to have men spend their strength outside of her field, and do nothing in her pressing work; to take what she can find as she waits by the wayside; to receive the leisure moments, and the money which is not otherwise bestowed, and the thought which cannot be more pleasantly employed — content while she fails in her direct work, because she is doing good incidentally. Till others agree to this method, she will continue to ask that religious service be made an essential part of the leading design of life.

It is evident that if the wayside work is merely accidental, there is no merit in it. The birds are gainers, and the man a loser. If we have done things reluctantly, begrudging the fowls the seed they bore away, we have little right to congratulate ourselves upon that which has been accomplished. Still, there is pleasure in thinking that we have done good in spite of ourselves, and we may make the good our own by rejoicing in it after the deed. But what we ought to do is to take this wayside work into our original plan; to mean to do good incidentally, beyond the main track of life. When we sow the fields for the harvest we ought to throw some seed to the birds, and to save seed and time for this.

> Thyself and thy belongings
> Are not thine own so proper, as to waste
> Thyself upon thy virtues, they on thee.
> Heaven doth with us as we with torches do,
> Not light them for themselves; for if our virtues
> Did not go forth of us, 'twere all alike
> As if we had them not.

All things come in fittingly when the life is sound and true. The highest end a man can serve is to please God. To this he should be always and in all things devoted. He can do for himself and for men and birds nothing better than to please God. In his Providence every way has its wayside. If we cannot spend all our time in giving cups of water to the thirsty, and befriending the friendless, we can spend a part of our time in such employment. The Master gives us spare hours which belong in the very substance of our life, and are accepted by Him whose are the birds. In all the stress of common life we have now and then a holiday. It would indeed be hard if religion gave us no leisure for anything beyond saying our prayers and saving our souls. We shall do most for ourselves when we have others in our plans. There is nothing better for the poor than that our care for them lie within a purpose which moves on to him who was rich and for the poor's sake became poor.

He has taught us usefulness as a vital part of piety. He has made us with different measures of ability that all kinds of good service may be done. Some have five talents and some one. This is not chance. In its own place the one is as five, for it is complete. Out of their place the five are as one.

In some places the man of stout arm is better than he of strong brain. The owner of a thousand acres might not feed the birds so well as a farmer's boy. And the birds must be fed. So God makes farmers' boys. They may own the acres at last. The final honors and rewards will be properly bestowed.

> Spirits are not finely touched
> But to fine issues.

He who in the parable did not count the hours of work when he paid the laborers may not make much account of talents in the last award. Every good and faithful servant shall be satisfied when he enters into the joy of his Lord. It is well to know what we can do best and are sent to do, and to do it willingly unto the Lord. When Brunelleschi surprised and delighted his rival with the crucifix which he had carved, Donatello frankly exclaimed, " I see truly that you are made for Christ's, and my art is fit for nothing more than peasants." The happy thing is, that both could work for Christ.

It is essential that life be given to the noblest end; man can do something better than to feed birds. or rather he can include that in a greater work. This he must do. Nothing is large enough for a man except religion. This contains virtue and the virtues. Love, not labor, is the fulfilling of the law. The faith which saves is a faith which works. We want the revolving wheel, but we want also the stream behind it and the loom before it. Religion moving the life to a holy end makes a manly character, which is free and eternal.

Put the best seed in the best ground for Christ's sake — your best seed in your best ground — and the harvest will come, and there will be seed by the wayside for the birds. More will come to them, take the years together, than if you thought only of the birds, and cast the seed only at the roadside.

We must secure good seed, and sow it carefully, and gather in prudently, or soon there will be no grain for either man or bird. The best material for usefulness God furnishes to the obedient. We need broad and long views, if we are to do our work and bless the world. The greatest interest should not be forgotten because smaller ones are close at hand. It is neither just nor kind; neither reverent nor benevolent. One of our wise men said in the college chapel, "My friends, as a general rule we are not wont to trifle with our important temporal interests; let us not trifle with our moral and religious interests merely because they are eternal." We are able to bring to the illustrating of this theme that life which here, with us, has fulfilled its course and met with its transition.

A good and useful man has been taken from us.* You will say that it is right to commend a career like his; and the more fitting that it was not remote from the opportunities of other men. It is well that our young men should see the reward which crowns fidelity, honesty, industry, economy; which from a small beginning makes a large ending. It is well that busy men should see how one can be very busy and very successful, and still maintain his interest in the church which holds his vows, and reserve time for its service of prayer and devout counsel. His works here were

* Mr. E. P. Whitman.

on a liberal scale, and stand conspicuous in the day long to be remembered within these gates, the day of our great rejoicing. The initials of his name are cut on yonder capital. Yet not in such special, deliberate acts of generosity only, but in the daily, unrecorded deeds which enrich a life, did he abound. With a wise foresight and a clear purpose, he cast good seed into good furrows, and the harvest came in a hundred-fold. But he never forgot the birds. The wayside was parallel to the furrows, and some seed fell there. For many a year the birds will sing sweetly above his grave. "Inasmuch as ye have done it unto one of the least of these" — He did it to the least, and to the most. He rests; but his works follow in the path and along the wayside where he trod. "Behold a sower went forth to sow: Whatsoever a man soweth that shall he also reap."

This parable of the sower our Lord applied to himself and his own work. "He that soweth the good seed is the Son of Man." His reference to the seed by the wayside was not directly for the purpose to which it has been applied this morning. Yet it was preëminently true of his life that it had its twofold influence, the direct and the incidental. He came with a large and divine intent; with one work to be done in one way. It was a very broad work. He filled all the land with blessing. He healed the sick and raised the dead. He taught the noblest principles of conduct and exemplified them in his own life. He sent the benison of his presence into countless homes, and gave his benediction to more children than he folded in his arms. He taught virtue to the world. He enriched humanity by his incarnation. The glistening of his garments has made the earth bright. "Take that name out of the world," said Theodore Parker, "that great character out of the world, and all its influence, and what should we be? I speak within bounds when I say he has advanced the civilization of the world at least a thousand years." He did more than that. He made our civilization, which before him gave no sign of even being. He makes everything live whither he comes. The blessings which crowd and crown our lives bear the image and superscription of the Christ. Do we think of it, that liberty and peace and home; intelligence, manhood, happiness, are not Saxon, but Christian?

Jerusalem is the mother of us all. Above Bethlehem our fathers saw the great light. From the land in which the Christ lived and taught, and wrought his miracles, and gave himself as the Redeemer of men, has come the light which is lighting the world. This is history. He who traces liberty and humanity to their birthplace comes to what was indeed the Land of Promise. The language of the prophet has been, is being, fulfilled in the advance of a pure Christianity. "And it shall come to pass, that everything that liveth, which moveth, whithersoever the rivers shall come, shall live." The Christ made, and is making, into a living and divine reality, the words of the prophet which he read in the synagogue of Nazareth, with the spirit of the Lord upon him, and good tidings flowing from his lips.

It might seem that this work was enough for the Son of Man. Let him accomplish this and receive the homage of the world! But we know from his own lips that it was not for this he came into the world. This is the birds' portion; the seed by the wayside. All this is within that which is greater. He came that men might have life, and have life more abundantly. He worked wonders, and his benign influence has never left the world. But his eye and his heart have been always on something beyond. Standing among his miracles, he said: "I have a baptism to be baptized with; and how am I straitened till it be accomplished." It was to redeem men that he came; to give his life a ransom for many. "Christ Jesus came into the world to save sinners." Prophets and apostles, men like Moses and Joshua, like Paul and John; or if men failed, angels could have taught the world, set a pure example, made homes and schools and churches; brought liberty and culture. This needed not the incarnation of God, the long humiliation, the sacrifice on Calvary. Angels might bring down the celestial torches, and change night into day. But an archangel could not redeem a soul; could not purchase pardon by the offering of himself; could not loose the bands of a double death, and open before the guilty the gates of immortality. An angel could teach men; only Christ could die for men. Only he could be the Redeemer, the Saviour, the Mediator. For this he bowed the heavens and came down; for this he walked the weary way to his cross and sepulchre. He fed the birds as he passed on; but he passed on, for he had come to die, and he pressed forward to that. He began to tell his disciples that he should suffer and be killed, and one rebuked him: "Be it far from thee, Lord; this shall not be unto thee." He turned to that man and said, "Get thee behind me, Satan: thou art an offence unto me: for thou savorest not the things that be of God."

The thought, the love, the sacrifice, blessed men here, but ran far out through the world and beyond it; beyond the bounds of time; beyond the burning of the earth, and the flaming heavens shriveling "like a parched scroll;" into the new heaven and the new earth, and adown the endless ages; and the blessings which he came to make for men, beginning here, were to be there forever. This is the work of Christ in the world: this eternal redemption, the bestowment of unceasing mercies upon men, by his grace the sons and heirs of God.

It is in comparison to this, the real intent, the grand accomplishment, that his other work,

magnificent and gracious as it is, beyond all
men's, I have ventured to call incidental, service by the way, the feeding of the birds. And
I believe that in saying this I have the mind of
Christ. One thing is certain, that what he
enjoined upon us especially to remember, and
even embodied in a sacrament that we might keep
it in constant and clear remembrance, was — not
his miracles, his teachings, his example; but this
— his redemption of the world by the offering up of
himself, the Lamb of God. We treasure his words,
and we repeat his life; but he said, "Except ye
eat the flesh of the Son of Man and drink his blood,
ye have no life in you."

I might leave this subject to suggest its own
lessons. Yet suffer me to call to your mind two
practical thoughts: The first is, that we must be
careful fully to teach the reality of his work. His
one work, his inclusive work, we must show to
men. We must constantly keep in mind for what
he came into the world. All that was related to
this should be taught so far as we have opportunity; but the chief work must be told, illustrated, enforced, till it becomes a part of the life
and character which we are shaping. The geography of Palestine is of small account unless we
become followers of Him who brightened snowy
Hermon with his presence, honored Nazareth and
Capernaum by his residence, hallowed Bethlehem
and Bethany, and was at Jerusalem one greater

than the Temple. The miracles of Christ have but a transient use unless through them we see him who by these signs showed Himself able to do greater things; who is himself the wonder of the ages; in whose works among men there is no marvel equal to his incarnation and resurrection; no might to be compared with the strength of his love. We shall repeat his precepts and enjoin obedience. We shall describe the beauty and purity of his life, till words fail us. We shall say that life is to be saved by losing it, and that our highest honor is in ministering to others. While time lasts we shall repeat these things. When philosophy has grown weary of teaching virtue, the Church will continue her lessons, ceasing not before Christ comes again. But in all this we have not taught Christ himself. He was more than this. He did more than this. He is the Saviour, and it is Christ the Saviour whom we must see and show. It is faith in him, and love for him, which we must enjoin, and the life lived by faith and love.

Let me take counsel with you, for you know men. I never speak to a man who is not before long to quit the world and find the judgment. What shall I say to men? Is it incidental or essential mercy which will serve them now and to the end? Sometimes the issue is imminent. I stand at the bedside of a dying man. His minutes are few, and the minister's words must be brief. They must be true words, fitly spoken.

The fading tapestry of a human life needs apples of gold. Shall I read the Sermon on the Mount to his cold, dull ears, or answer the pleading of his eyes with maxims of morality? Should I not rather follow the divine example, and turn the anxious gaze to God in penitence and love, putting upon his faltering lips the cry of his brother publican — "God be merciful "— "be merciful to me?" Should I not teach him another prayer, which brought its answer of mercy —" Lord remember me?" From the broken and contrite heart let these petitions rise, with mind and heart clinging to him who taught them to men. If he is saved it is Christ himself who saves him; who died for him — died for him.

The man who suffered at our Saviour's side, who from the cross followed him that day into Paradise, had heard little in his wild career of the teachings of Jesus, so pure and blessed; had seen, it may be, not one of his works of mercy; but in that awful moment he saw Christ; he knew his righteousness; he proclaimed his royalty; he committed himself to him; he lifted up his voice in confession, — and it was the only voice there which did confess him, — and the lost sheep, bruised, and torn, and bleeding, died on the Shepherd's shoulder and found life. The Christ whom he knew, and the Christ whom he trusted, the Christ who saved, was in literal truth Christ crucified. Wherever this Gospel is preached, and this story is told of a man who was saved, the world will see that it was Christ on the cross who saved; it was the hands that were made strong by the nails which opened the celestial gates to a ransomed soul, who fled from the body of death into the embrace of life.

The other thought is kindred to this. We are to have the man's portion of Christ's words; not the birds' alone. The incidental benefits of our Lord's life are too great for us; are not great enough for us, seeing that he is Christ. It is not the desert of the receiver, but the grace of the giver, which makes the gift. We should be grateful for the crumbs; yet he calls us to the feast. We are not birds who must needs take what we chance to find, but God's children, in his house, in his love, wayward and hungry, but his children still; and we can choose and take his best gifts. If we open our heart under the sower's hand the choicest wheat will fall and keep falling upon us. The wisdom of Christ was great in his parables; it was at its height in his death. His power was wonderful in his miracles; it was at its best in his crucifixion. His grace was large in his patience, his comfort, his sympathy, his help. It was boundless when he gave himself to the cross for our sake. We can have him at his best; his wisest wisdom, his strongest strength, his divinest grace. The larger holds the large; Christ redeeming is Christ teaching, healing, blessing, enlarged. We can have the best and the whole, the Christ who is enthroned above, the temple and the light of heaven; the royal Lamb, the Redeemer-King. To Him must we look; to the real Saviour, as he really saves. When we have found him we have found life. From the good ground we are shall spring up the good seed he sows, and our life shall be fruitful; a delight to us, a gladness to the world, a glory to him.

Thus once again the sower sows the seed. May the birds be the richer for it — the birds and the men.

XV.

TRUTH COMMENDING ITSELF.

SCRIPTURE LESSON: *I. Cor.* i: 17-31.

TEXT: By manifestation of the truth commending ourselves to every man's conscience in the sight of God. *II. Cor.* iv: 2.

THIS was a noble confidence. It was a personal confidence. This man, called to do a work which before his time had not been done in the world, had that assurance which comes from the belief that one is doing the will of God, and the additional conviction that he is also approving himself to men; that he is not only serving God, but serving men; that he has the commendation of every man's conscience, when that conscience is in the presence of God. Manifestly it was upon this that this man must rely in his work. He could not compel men; he had no devices by which he could attract them. He could simply tell them the truth as it was committed to him. If it did not commend itself to their consciences, it was spoken in vain. If he had been willing by any other methods to attract them — for doubtless he might have gathered a school if he would, and have gained many followers — still he would not have accomplished his purpose unless he had gained the conscience of those whom he taught, because his work must needs be done in the hearts of men, where their motives, and purposes, and character are made up.

The apostle is speaking here in words of great strength, which suggest two lines of commendation. In the first place, the gospel itself, the substance of it, commends itself to every man's conscience. Secondly, in its method, in the manner of its presentation, the gospel commends itself to the consciences of men. It is upon this latter fact rather than upon the former, that I shall speak to you this morning; that the method of the gospel commends itself to every man's conscience, when that conscience is face to face with God.

There are three grand words here, around which the life of this man formed itself. *God, conscience, truth;* God above, conscience within, truth between, touching God on the upper side of it; touching man on the lower side of it, and in this trinity of God, conscience, truth, God's purposes are accomplished in the world, and man's redemption is secured.

What do we mean by the gospel? It is briefly expressed in that evangel which lies within the evangel: "God so loved the world that he gave his Son." Upon this our faith and our preaching rest.

The design of the gospel is so to control men's lives and thoughts that they shall be in right relations with God; that it shall be as true that they are God's children as that he is their father; that they shall be loving and obedient children, and shall receive his continual care and all the blessings of his affection; and the manner in which this truth comes to us commends itself to the conscience of men.

Let me ask you, then, to notice these things. In the first place, if there be any such gospel as this, manifestly the very first thing in it — that which cannot be left out, that which cannot be changed though everything else were changed — the first thing is that the gospel shall be from God. It is grace, God's grace; it is forgiveness, God's forgiveness. It is the restoration to right relations with God, and these God must determine; it is the entrance of man into God's house and into his heart. Evidently, then, the gospel must be divine; it must come from above. However much men may think, and desire, and believe, nothing has any authority until God gives it. The common word "testament" carries this idea. A testament is a will. The value of the will is in the signature. It may be drawn by the best lawyer in the land; it may be filled with the most generous and judicious provisions; it may be engrossed upon the finest parchment by the most skilful penman in the world; yet it is only worth so much as the bare parchment is worth until the man who owns the property signs it. It is so with this New Testament. St. Paul could not make it; no man, not all men together, could make it; the thoughts of men are not to be trusted, until God, with his own hand, writes his name. This should be clearly understood, because so often men think that they can make a gospel; that they can reason it out, or that it can spring up within them. We can determine the kind of will our rich neighbor ought to make, but he does not always make the sort of will we should have written. God makes his own testament, and not until he signs it is it a testament.

Then, again, it must have its human side. If this is the redemption of men, it must come to men; it must enter into them and be wrought out among them. We can see how fitting and necessary it is that there should be one among men, having their form and estate, living before them the life that God's children ought to lead; illustrating his righteousness, declaring his grace, and proving its power and simplicity in his own open experience. We are convinced that the gospel must have its human as well as its divine side.

I do not know that we should have thought this out, yet it seems probable that we should have planned it somewhat in this way, because these two ideas have entered into the religious thought of different natures. They have believed that God has come down among men, and has lived and worked in human form. This gospel which St. Paul preached is divine; the word that was in the beginning with God and was God, has made it and taught it. It is human; the divine word was made flesh and dwelt among men, and we have seen his glory. Must a gospel be divine? Christ is divine. Must a gospel be human? Christ is human. To create and bestow the gospel God was manifest in the flesh. In this the gospel commends itself to us.

But passing from this, it is reasonable to expect that a gospel coming to men will be preached by men; that it will not be written upon the heavens, or declared by mystic signs among the stars. God works by men. Every nation has its prophet. It seems to be one of the primal and essential thoughts of men that if God ever speaks to the world, he will speak by men. Hence when this gospel comes by men it uses the most natural method. The most simple way in which God can speak to the world, is by speaking to certain men and letting them utter the truth to the nations. That is the method of the gospel. If we take the life of that apostle who more than any other has been the minister of God's gospel to the world, we see how this truth is fulfilled, so that the life of St. Paul may be considered a part of the method of the gospel.

If you examine the life of this man you will see how wonderfully suited he was to this work. He belonged in the world. He had a rare advantage in that he was of Hebrew parentage while he was a Roman citizen. He was not born in Italy nor in Palestine, but between the two, in the Asiatic province of Cilicia. He was a man of great ability; a man of learning, trained in all which the schools of Tarsus could teach him, and in that special instruction which was given at Jerusalem. A man of great sincerity and fidelity; of great independence and generosity; a man just and faithful, disposed to give himself in all sacrifice and devotion for men; tender, tearful — the tears of St. Paul, which he confesses, are one of his marked characteristics — a man of patriotism, with an unchanging attachment to his own people; thoroughly, at first narrowly, religious and determined to have a conscience void of offence in the sight of God and men.

This is the man who comes to us with the gospel of God; a man who stood so near to Christ and those who were the closest to him, that he could almost hear his words as they were spoken. A man who had come into this truth by a profound personal experience; who was not called upon to give to others that which he had not felt himself. He came through that humbling way by which publicans must come, tearing himself from the associations and hopes of his life, and giving himself up to one who had no renown, and upon whose cross there rested not that glory, which, looking back, we now can discern.

This man, with these personal traits, and this personal experience, went to Corinth, and is going through the world, declaring the truths of the gospel of Christ. I do not say that the gospel is true because St. Paul preached it, but I do say that it is a very strong testimony to the truth of the gospel that St. Paul believed it. The man gives weight to his belief. The value and the validity of a lawyer's, a physician's, a philosopher's, a mechanic's judgment depends greatly upon the character and knowledge of the man. This man, in all the strength and sublimity and simplicity of his character, stands forth as a personal witness to a gospel which had satisfied his conscience, had met the wants of his life, had rewarded him for his sacrifice, had given him assurance in his work, and fortitude and cheerfulness in imprisonment and under the shadow of a cruel death.

Thus the gospel, coming to us with its divine and human character, and coming to us in this personal method, commends itself to every man's conscience.

I might add to this the lives of the other apostles, who were men standing near to Christ and who received the gospel in such a way that it changed their life, and made them give their testimony to its truth, even in loss and death. I might bring to your notice the list of men in later times — wise and saintly men; confessors and martyrs — who have taken this truth to prove it under all varieties and conditions of life, and who, having satisfied themselves of its power, have become the ministers of it to others.

I might present to you the long catalogue of the noble and the good, the wise and the brave; the men who have done most to dignify and ennoble humanity; men whose lives for purity never have been exceeded, whose spirit for nobility never has been excelled; who confess before us that the gospel meets all the requirements of their nature, and enables them cheerfully to become its witnesses to the conscience of men through all the world. But upon this I cannot dwell.

Let me ask you to notice, in the third place, that this gospel comes to us — it is a part of the method of it — not imposing upon us a bald authority, silencing our questions, bidding us commit ourselves blindly to a wisdom which is above us. It comes answering our questions; even starting new questions, that may it answer them. It does not say of any anxious inquiry of the soul, "This is not for you to know; this is for your masters, and for the priests." It solves questions of profound import which are answered nowhere else. We stand among mysteries, are full of inquiries. A man's relation to God, a man's duty, the way of restoration to God which shall give him peace and assurance; a man's destiny and the way to make that destiny blessed — upon these themes the world has no clear voice, save where the gospel is preached. I wander from man to man with the serious thoughts which come to me, as I know that in a few years, at the most, I shall go hence. But no man tells me anything much better than I have thought out by myself. I stand among the open graves of your households, to hear you ask, "What is there beyond?" And all the schools are silent; the oracles are dumb. We utter our hope through our tears; the untaught centuries have added nothing to the human hopes. Knowledge was never so great as to-day; the pursuit of knowledge was never so vigorous; but all the study has not added a syllable which answers the questions which we must have answered; for whose answer we would be willing to deny ourselves much which men call knowledge.

This silence is significant when knowledge is so vast and is growing on every hand. Men are bringing the heavens down to the earth, and walking along their streets they are wakening the strong forces of forgotten generations, and their life flies through the air and swims through the sea as if it had not been dead for ages. Men are studying their own thoughts, and philosophy was never so venturesome, perhaps never so wise, as it is to-day. I can know almost anything that I want to know.

Nothing is so distant in space or so remote in time that I may not hope to know of it all which I need to know. With this knowledge rising about my feet, until I am half drowned with the mere names of the topics which it presents to me, I ask if there is nothing to be known of the things which are most important. I go through the libraries from shelf to shelf, from book to book, and they tell me almost everything but that which I must know. I press my inquiries and beg for a reply, and the wise men say, "We will teach you everything else; we will tell you what you sprung from; we will analyze your character; we will break the light into fragments and lay the stars as a glittering dust at your feet; but your duty you cannot know; your relation to God you cannot know; what comes after death you cannot know; the way of bringing peace to your conscience and righteousness to your life you cannot know." I say that *we can know*. In the name of growing, star-eyed science, we can know. In the name of fourteen hundred students in our university, we can know. In the name of our vast libraries, our bold search for truth, our accumulated, teeming, and overwhelming knowledge of everything else, *we can know*. I know that I can know. God, duty, life, destiny — I am sure that I can know them; and I find the knowledge in this gospel of God, which answers the questions with a voice that does not tremble; which gratifies this longing of the heart to whom these are the real, the practical things of life; and because the gospel comes to me doing what must be done, telling what I must know, supplementing all the growing knowledge of the world, it commends itself to my conscience in the sight of God. My conscience says that I can know my duty and my destiny. The world says, "We cannot tell you your duty nor your destiny." The gospel says, "I tell you your duty and your destiny;" and my conscience smiles upon the revelation and glories in it.

In its rational method the gospel commends itself to the conscience. It addresses itself at once to the spirit. It recognizes the spiritual nature of man. That grand sentence, almost the grandest sentence in the Bible, which our Saviour uttered at the well of Samaria, when he said, "God is a spirit," finds its counterpart in another truth implied all through the Scriptures. It might be rendered in this way: Man is a spirit, and they that help him must help him in spirit and in truth. Some persons, claiming our respect, say, man is a spirit, and they that help him must build him a better house; they must give him a better social estate; they must provide a better government; they must invent a new kind of sepulchre. But the gospel is better; it goes directly to the spirit of man. That word "conscience" itself is a witness. What other system of religion clearly pronounces the word? What system of learning speaks the word " conscience " except as it takes it from the gospel? To the reason, to the affections, to the will — that is, to the man himself, Scripture appeals. It flashes no sword; it stretches out no sceptre; it paints no picture; it sings no song; it raises no glittering pageant which may delight and bewilder. It comes with the simple truth to the reason and heart of man. You may hear this truth of God in the stateliest cathedral with all the accompaniments of architecture and music. You may hear it in the camp of the soldier. The sailor may read it in his forecastle. The wrecked mariner may recall it upon the ocean rock. The prisoner may remember it in the dungeon. The dying man may catch its words from the scroll at the foot of his bed. You may not have the book; you may recall but a single chapter, a single sentence of it; and that sentence in its witness to God, and duty, and truth, and redemption, shall be enough to save a man into a righteous life and to give him a glorious hope. In this independence of all things that are without; in this method of finding no heart in our solitude, the gospel commends itself. When you want to think well on a subject, you wish to be alone. You do not ask the architect to make a cathedral so great that its inspiration shall help you in your hard thinking. You do not ask the singers to sing to you a song that shall bring to you a better revelation of your duty in some practical matter of daily life. You say, leave me alone. Our best thinking, I suppose, is done when the lights are out and the city around us is still. If I am to think upon my duty, I want to think in silence. My reason must be quick; my conscience must waken; I must not be disturbed; the truth must come to me in such a form that I can take and hold it in my mind without a book, and ponder it without a preacher. This gospel which brings itself so quietly to my solitude, commends itself to me. If we cannot be saved until we have trodden the temples of the old world; if we cannot be saved until the most majestic music bears our worship to the skies, there is little hope for us. But a gospel which you can teach your children, which you can repeat to yourselves as you walk the streets, which in the sanctity and repose of your own minds you can dwell upon and work into your life, is a gospel which commends itself to the good sense of a man in the sight of God. All the record is open; the Church has not a single secret; we keep nothing back; we tell the whole that is given to us for our guidance, and we pray men to search the Scriptures, that they may determine whether their gospel commends itself to every man's conscience in the sight of God.

The gospel comes to us in this way to give us a standard of life. It does not leave us to evolve out of our own consciousness the principles of duty. It sets before us a rule; an ideal to which we are to attain. It honors conscience in doing this. It honors conscience, again, because it does not give to us the details of life. It would simplify duty if a few volumes not much larger than this Bible were written, in which all things that men are likely to think of doing could be catalogued, and numbered, and classified, so that the glance of the eye would show us what to do.

How simple a thing it would be in the practical questions of ethics, for one to turn to the book, and find the column over which is written the name of that which he is thinking about, and then find at once whether it is right for him to do it or not! Now, the gospel pursues a different method. It gives to us certain principles which respect our conscience and our reason; and it leaves reason to judge of these things and to apply them. It leaves conscience to determine how this law shall be laid upon our life. Conscience likes this treatment. A man wants to be out of leading strings. We like to think that God has given us a real liberty, and that he has not told us in precise and minute terms what we are to do between twelve and one o'clock to-day, and between one and two o'clock to-morrow; that he lets us decide these matters for ourselves. Conscience likes this, and approves the gospel which leaves to it its proper work. But the gospel gives to us certain general maxims, and these conscience approves. I need not repeat them now. One or two of them I may mention: "Whatsoever a man soweth, that shall he also reap," which is one of the fundamental principles of the gospel. Every man says that is right. "He that soweth bountifully shall reap also bountifully; and he that soweth sparingly shall reap also sparingly." And this: "Every man shall give account of himself to God." And this: "It is more blessed to give than to receive." I might enlarge the list; I think that every one of them commends itself to us. We desire to have every one of them applied by our neighbors, and sometimes consent that they should be applied by ourselves. And if there be any rules which seem to reach above us to-day, we remember that we are going on into a world where these same relations are to hold good. The Sermon on the Mount, in its essential principles, is as true in heaven as it is upon earth, and will always be true. If we cannot come to the mastery of all its rules to-day, perhaps we can to-morrow.

Then, again, in laying down certain principles which are to govern our life, the gospel enjoins duties which human commandments could not require. No commandment could require you to love your child. It could prevent your abuse of him; it could require you to instruct him; but it could not require you to love him. No statute could make you forgive a man who had wronged you. It could prevent your striking him, perhaps, but the gospel enjoins love and forgiveness. God administers the gospel upon principles of equity, which are beyond statutes; and in doing this it commends itself to our conscience.

But advancing once more, the gospel commends itself to a man's conscience by the way in which it regards a man. We are sensitive, and we ought to be. The gospel treats a man with respect. I should like to repeat that, because this method is not always followed: The gospel treats manhood with great respect. It does not try to drive him; it does not scold him; it does not denounce him and call him by opprobrious epithets. It never once forgets that a man is a child of God; it never overlooks the fact that a man is to live forever. It finds the column of the temple lying in the dust and the sand driven over it. But it does not call it rubbish; it calls it a column; a fallen column. It rebuilds the temple out of this single shaft; it marks the beauty of the material, the sublimity of the proportions, the very carving and tracery of the shattered capital, and seeks to raise it up and to construct a house around it. The gospel speaks of man as fallen; but it is man who has fallen; and fallen man has conscience, and reason, and will, and the love of God, and the endless years. It calls man dead in trepasses and sins; but it offers to this man eternal life. It pronounces him guilty; it proffers to him righteousness. I ask you if all the books of men treat our common manhood with that respect and dignity with which the gospel always treats it.

Then it deals impartially with us; it makes no account of race, or class, or estate. It treats every man in his own personality. It never confuses men one with another. It respects conscience with such decrees as this: "Who art thou that judgest another man's servant? To his own master he standeth or falleth." We like that sentence. We are glad to know that when we stand before God we shall not be judged for the deeds of our ancestors, or the deeds of our neighbors. Only my own life have I to answer for. For its shortcomings I must be judged; for its repentance I may be accepted. Solitary and alone a man may be in his piety, but he shall have that piety remembered in the Day. Independent individual, free, with his freedom always kept in mind, the man is judged by the law of liberty. I know that I do what I choose to do; I feel that it is right that God should judge me by that which I choose to do. It is a cardinal principle of the gospel, and conscience pronounces it just. Indeed, conscience wanders along these lines of divine truth, and pausing at every sentence, gives its approval: "That is right; that is just; that is true." From first to last the principles of God's government, the principles of God's grace, are just. If I fall beneath them, they are just. If, to give account of the deeds which I am doing is my ruin, it is just that I should give an account of the deeds which I am doing. The work of the gospel is thorough upon both sides; thorough upon the side of its law, its assertion of principle; thorough upon that which it calls us to do. It respects man by making man to bear his part in the work of his own redemption. Redemption is a common word in the Scriptures, but it is not more common than repentance. We are told that we have gone away from God. We are told of the regeneration of God's Spirit; but we are bidden to make to ourselves a new heart and a new spirit. We are told of Christ's salvation, but not as if we were to be driven into Paradise because Christ has died. It is as thorough upon this side when it says, " Work out your own salvation, for it is God which worketh in you." The gospel which brings to me the assured truth of God and the assured truth of my own life and duty, commends itself to my conscience. I believe, if I am saved, it is because of Christ's redemption; I believe, if I am saved by Christ's redemption, it is because I repent of my sins and trust him. I believe that I have the salvation of Christ; I believe that I must work out my own salvation. And it is in this thoroughness, this breadth, this largeness of its assertion, that the gospel commends itself to the conscience of a thoughtful man.

Brethren, there are many more things which might be presented, upon which I cannot detain you now. If this which I have said is true, it will be found true when you have gone to your homes, and when you think upon it by the way. If the gospel is that which St. Paul claimed it to be, it will commend itself to your conscience. I do not know what you will do with it. You may not submit your life to it; you may disown it; you may reject its duties and its graces. But if it is God's gospel, your conscience will say that it is right. So kind is it, so helpful, speaking great words of us, and starting great hopes for us. How it raises us up, and makes our manhood vast and eternal, and brings to us the beginning of an endless destiny, whose glories we can only dimly see while upon their shadowy confines we are waiting. Brethren, I cannot answer for you; you do not need it, nor wish it. A man must be the judge for himself. One thing I know: It is no hasty thought; it is no narrow opinion, after a brief, contracted, uneventful experience. One thing I know: that the gospel of Christ commends itself to my conscience as I stand here in the sight of God. I could not describe myself so well as the Bible has described me. No one will ever care to write the story of my life; but no man ever could write it as it is written here. I have lived through almost all the Bible, and the rest is not far distant. It tells the truth about me; it answers every question I ask which is of great account; it satisfies the longings which I have to know; it gives me wise counsel for my duty. I never yet have been sorry when I have done as it told me; I have been sorry a thousand times when I have not obeyed it. In my most quiet hours, in the hours when I have seen my kindred fall into the grave, in view of all that is before me, I have found it true. I say here in the sight of Almighty God, my conscience is satisfied with the gospel of Christ.

XVI.

THE POWER OF AN ENDLESS LIFE.

[Preached at Wellesley College.]

SCRIPTURE LESSON : *Hebrews* vii: 16.

TEXT: Who is made, not after the law of a carnal commandment, but after the power of an endless life. *Hebrews* vii: 16.

THIS was said of the Lord Jesus Christ. When he came into the world to be our great High Priest, he did not make up his life after an earthly standard, suiting himself to the priesthood, and the priestly service, and the fashion of things which he found among men ; but he had regard to that which was permanent, and set his life into endless proportions. He did not adapt himself to Solomon's temple, but to the temple's Solomon. He knew that in a few years the temple and the city which it adorned would be removed. Men were to be independent of place and time, and were to worship God in spirit and in truth. The worship was to be forever. He saw the endless life of man, and in all his plan and work addressed himself to this, and made up his purposes and gave himself to the world as its Redeemer, after the power of an endless life. It behooved him to do this because the life of man is endless. That which is limited in its ability and design cannot meet the requirements of one whose years are boundless. He needs an "eternal redemption" and an "everlasting gospel." He has all which he needs in the power of the endless life of Christ.

There is a profound and practical truth here for our own governance. Man is to make up his thought and plan, his purpose and will, and to do his work, not by the law of that which is transient, but by the power of that which is eternal. He has an endless life, and in the sight of that fact he is to live. He is not to fit himself to a world which he will presently desert, or to adopt the maxims and methods of a temporary system, or to set a limit to his years, and mistake a change of his place for a change of himself. He is to have it constantly in mind that he is to live for uncounted years, and to govern himself in accordance with this reality. Not a carnal, earthly, perishing commandment, but the power of an endless life, is to rule his intent and his deed.

I do not know where these things could be said more fittingly than here. We read the lesson a few months ago in connection with the birthday of the man who founded this college. We read it again on the first anniversary of his translation.

This is his real birthday, so he would have said. It is this which we are taught in the New Testament, where small account is made of our entrance into this world, and little is said of that which we call death, with the knell, the pall, the bier; but the great event is the going on to Christ when his prayer is answered: "Father, I will that they also whom thou hast given me be with me where I am." It is rather the beginning than the ending of a life which is in our minds to-night. He was not planning for the years during which he might continue here. He cast his work far in advance. He made it a part of an endless plan. He knew that he was to be, not for seventy years, but for seventy thousand years, and he measured his purposes by that standard. He began a work which was to endure. To erect buildings was merely incidental to his design. He proposed to build characters. He formed a home and a school for those who were to live through the ages, and he arranged the institution around that idea. He brought together teachers who could instruct in the principles of everlasting life, and offered to the scholars wisdom which they could use at once, and use forever. The course of study covers seventy thousand years, and more. The buildings will fall, the earth itself will pass away, but the lessons will last. Truth is not held to times and things. This He knew well. It entered into his own life. He meant to have it enter the lives of others. In this stands the high renown of his purpose. He was wise when he invested his endless thought in an endless school. It remains to have this purpose recognized and fulfilled by all who enter these gates bringing in their endless years, that they may be inspired and controlled by the power of an endless life.

There is but one life in the world — it is the life of God. In him all life has its being. The life of man is at the first in the eternal purpose of the Creator. By that purpose man comes into his personal being Every one's genealogy ends like that given by St. Luke: "Which was the son of Adam, which was the son of God." A man is an eternal thought incarnate. The artist's thought precedes the picture and the song. This is after the pattern. One is "before all things, and in him all things consist." Endless life in God is a life of will and purpose. The true life of man contains the same will and intention. "Thy will be done," is not designed as an afterthought, but as the primal desire of the man. If he sets himself against God's purposes, he will be destroyed. If he attempts to stand still before them, he will be overwhelmed. If he makes his own purpose move on with them, he will have a prosperous career and an everlasting reward. The pagan likes to think of his divinities in repose. Jesus said, "My Father worketh even until now, and I work." He was able to say at length, "I glorified Thee on the earth, having accomplished the work which

Thou hast given me to do." We are to do our work, changing the thought of God into word and deed. It is in this that we have failed. The result is not measured by earthly years. To bring us into our place, to establish us in righteous lives, and make our being a blessing, the Christ has come and given himself for us. Henceforth we are to be followers of him, in the power of an endless life. Our thought for ourselves is to rise into Christ's thought for us.

Let us notice some things which will result from the persistent thought of our endless life.

I. It will give us a calmness of spirit and behavior. The work of the world is not all on us. The Lord reigns. We have our part of his will to do, and only that. There are many others who are working on the same plan. We begin our part of the work, but not the work itself. That begins in God. It is only our part which we end when we end anything; when we seem to leave our work that we may go hence. Oftentimes we see those into whose labors we are entering, with whom we shall rejoice in the harvest of our common life. We can often appoint those who shall carry forward our endeavor. We can train children and scholars to take our place. Moses was permitted to intrust his work to his friend Joshua. He could do this with great assurance because he knew the man. He could do it with joy, if he knew himself and the events before him. He was buried in a valley in the land of Moab, over against Beth-peor, and no man knew his sepulchre. Fifteen centuries went by, and again he was seen of men among the cliffs of Horeb, still engaged in his old work which was far advanced, when he talked with the Lord " of his decease which he was about to accomplish at Jerusalem." The passion of the soul may well be stilled when a man sees his centuries before him, and beholds the grandeur of his life. He will feel that he has time enough for all which he must do. Days are as many and as long as duties. He moves steadily forward, and finds that, if his wishes outgrow his time, his duty is well clothed upon. One of the wisest of our preachers and philosophers, whose life had been full of enterprise and rich in accomplishment, when he was near the change in his career, so that he could review his hurried past and look down the serene path before him, said, "If I had my life to live over again I would not push." There is little need of competition, and jealousy and jostling, when a man has endless years for his own, and with all other good men, is working out God's thought.

> All our bustling morrows only make
> The smooth to-day of God.

In the thought of his endless life he has comfort in his weariness and pain. Rest is coming. The good man's trouble is short-lived.

The morning's joy shall end the night of weeping,
And life's long shadows break in cloudless sun.

Men may have killed his body, but after that they have no more which they can do. He escapes their hand, and from the heights looks down on their baffled rage. This independence which belongs with immortality is rich in consolation. It gives courage and patience and triumph. No wonder martyrs sing at the stake, rejoicing that they are "counted worthy to suffer dishonor for the name." They know what is before them. It was not Wickliffe, but the dust he had worn, which went by the Avon and the Severn to the sea.

A man can bear all things which have a speedy end. He should be master of himself and of the world. It is a small matter that he is obscure and has no honor of his fellows; that he holds no land in the country through which he is passing, and has no house; that his work is humble and hard. If in his dark and lowly place he is working on the endless plan which God has committed to him, which soon will lead him into the kindly light, it is enough. He is quiet and hopeful. He waits upon the Lord and his will, and trusts the endless years:

Thus did he live his life,
A kind of passive strife,
Upon the God within his heart relying;

> Men left him all alone,
> Because he was unknown,
> But he heard the angels sing when he was dying.
>
> God judges of a light
> Which baffles mortal sight,
> And the useless seeming man the crown hath won:
> In his vast world above,
> A world of broader love,
> God hath some grand employment for his Son.

II. The power of the endless years will, also, have a stimulating, quickening influence. A large work whose results are of importance, furnishes an incentive to action. We do not wish to exert ourselves for that which is small. In the easy lesson, the simple problem, there is nothing to stir our energy or excite our ambition. The architect will not put his skill into the rude building which will be taken down to-morrow. Set him to the construction of a cathedral, and you engage all the forces of his mind and heart, and the days and nights of years will be given to his work.

To arrange a school for summer study would be the pastime of a leisure evening when the day's work is done. To plan and found a college need the man's highest powers in their best estate, and the devotion will gladly be made.

To think that our life is endless, and that we are making its character and deed day by day, after the largest measures, starts the blood, gives vigor to the will and stability to the purpose. All that a man is he consecrates to the sublime accomplishment. The teacher's thought enlarges its proportions when he sees the endless lines of his instruction. The scholar presses with eager step and expanding heart over the boundless fields before him.

It is stimulating for a man to remember that his life is leagued with other lives which are advancing, with which his own vision and intention must keep pace. Still more are his desires excited and his designs enlarged by the knowledge that he is working out the endless thought of God; that his life is a part of God's eternity, and that he is created for a limitless career. To know that he is the child of God, that his life is planned and himself guided by God, that his work is a part of the eternal fabric which God's omnipotence is constructing, this makes a man conscious of the grandeur of being, of the greatness of the thought which is incarnate in his manhood. Can one think upon his endless life and bear the strain? I can understand the burden of one who said, " The thought that this frail being is never to end is so overwhelming that my only shelter is God's presence." That shelter is denied to no one. Within the calmness of God's eternity the man holds his endless years. But they are years of life. They are years of grand requisition. It has been truly said that when religion no longer requires that men shall attempt the impossible, it ceases to be religion. God's will is a long will. The principles of his government run on forever. His laws are everlasting. Into this stability the man is born. According to his day his strength shall be. With this provision he is to advance. He is inclined to look back and seek his origin. Divine providence and divine commandment bid him go forward. He is promised a spiritual body which shall endure. His spirit is immortal. His works shall follow and attend him. To know this is to be strong. It makes a man great to feel the power of his endless years.

III. Under this influence he makes his own plans large and long, and works them into a large life. It is doubtful if one can have a generous ambition who does not see an ample future and submit to its control. It is certain that the strong men have looked before them and have worked for the future. Cicero asked, "What will history say of me six hundred years hence? I am more afraid of that than of the chatter of my contemporaries." "I have had the year two thousand, and even the year three thousand, often in my mind," wrote Macaulay. A greater man than either, Gladstone, said, "The last, the severest, the surest, the most awful judge, is the compensating award of posterity." The power of the future upon character is marked, and the relation of character to the future is evident. "Immortality will come to such as are fit for it; and he who would be a great soul in future must be a great soul now." The thought of the future and its demands is a help in work. The lesson which seems needless may be indispensable at some time. The service that is not rewarded at once may be liberally paid for at a later day. The young lawyer, Daniel Webster, conducted a suit for a New Hampshire farmer, and his fee was less than the money he expended in his study of the case. Years afterwards the principle involved in it was needed in a cause of large proportions, and his ready application of it brought him his ample reward. He had made up his opinion and learning, not by the dimensions of a trifling dispute, but by the power of a long career in the law.

In gathering and employing our possessions, the power of the coming years is an advantage. We need to earn to-day more than we can use to-day, and to secure while on the earth more than we shall use upon the earth. If we were always to be here, our investments should be here. It were foolish to place all our goods in a world which we are presently to leave. The instability of wealth comes from putting it in unstable places. The present is continually slipping away. It is the future which stands. The earth vanishes, but the new earth remains. Our Lord pointed past the moth and rust and thief, and bade men lay up for themselves treasures in Heaven. They were to send them in advance of their own going. In this security is an incentive to labor for treasure and comfort which we can enjoy when our immediate gains have passed out of our sight. "Riches certainly make themselves wings; they fly away as an eagle toward Heaven;" in a sad tone, out of an experience of loss, are the ancient words repeated. But wherein lies the sadness? Can nothing fly but riches? It is with an exultant voice that the prophet cries, "They that wait upon the Lord shall renew their strength; they shall mount up with wings as eagles." If the men are flying in the same direction with their riches, the parting cannot be long. We can at least determine the direction of the two flights. It will be a help to us, if looking beyond the river, we turn our riches toward the land where we would dwell, and let them rise upon their strong wings, to meet us on the farther shore when we alight. To give our treasure into God's keeping is to have it through all changes. To use it for him is to enjoy it forever. To think of the permanence of riches will affect us well in our gaining and losing, and getting and giving.

It is not the thought of the endless years only which is given to us, but of the endless years in which God dwells, where his law rules and his grace abounds; where his children have their home in life and joy; where they see him, and are like him, because they see him as he is. They call him a pagan who wrote, "It is pleasant to die, if there be gods; and sad to live, if there be none." Say "God," and the sentence is sublime and profound in its truth.

The power of the endless years throws our life forward and upward. Time holds us less firmly. We rise into clearer air, and feel the breath from the supernal hills. We find relief from our questionings; the curious Whence changes to a hopeful Whither, and we hear the answer, see it, are inspired by it. We do not set the broken column or the inverted torch over the place where we are to lie. We see our life entering the heavens, and mingling its light with the brightness of the perfect day. We turn away from the deeds of darkness and walk in the light. We come to Him who is "the same yesterday, and to-day and forever," and in his promises find hope, in his mercy life. "Because I live, ye shall live also," he said. Among our graves he spoke: "I am the resurrection." He gives us more than the succession of years which is our certain birthright. He changes time to life, and transforms being into immortality. He taught his apostle to write, "The wages of sin is death; but the free gift of God is eternal life in Christ Jesus our Lord."

The power of an endless life is designed for us all. It has a marvellous influence upon the young. It teaches them to lay long plans not to be bounded by an earthly commandment, but to reach on for a thousand years. It incites them to choose a calling which will serve them through the centuries, in the training it gives them, the spirit it fosters, the good it accomplishes, the gains it secures. It encourages them in study with the assurance that the enlarged mind will be large for the occupation and delights of another world, and that the truths learned here will attend them there. It counsels them to adopt for their guidance here the principles which will be found in force beyond, where Gabriel and Michael are held by the same twofold law which here declares our duty; where the reaping is like the sowing; where it is more blessed to give than to receive; where all glorify God and accomplish the work which he gives them to do. It is grand, blessed, to be young; to be at the entrance of the years which reach across the world, and in the fullness of hope and promise to go forward in the power of an endless life. "I have written unto you, young men, because ye are strong."

To the old, also, is given the power of an endless life. Their years are not behind them. Their work is not completed. Their faces are not toward the sunset. The light from the long day shines upon their path, and their hope enters the city which hath foundation. This is the golden age of one who has lived by the power of an endless life. Let me read here the words of a good man who in the fullness of his years went on to God. He quotes the saying of Cicero, "An old man has nothing indeed to hope for; yet he is in so much the happier state than a young man, since he has already attained what the other only hopes for."

But this will hardly satisfy," he adds. Then he continues, "There is no ignoring, there is no concealing the inconveniences, the infirmities, which steal over us as we descend into the vale of years." We who saw him every day as he moved with labored step and bending form among us, knew what he meant. But we saw more than his infirmities. He saw more. "It is a great thing, for an old man to retain his faculties and his natural cheerfulness to the last. It is a great thing to keep up his interest in good objects, and in his favorite studies and pursuits. It is great thing to be surrounded by kind friends, and all the endearments and appliances of a happy home. But greater than all ' to know Christ, and the power of his resurrection,' as a hope full of immortality."

The last word of Harvard College to her sons as they go forth to their work, is the sentence of the Hebrew prophet which she has written upon her wall, which she would fain repeat in the ears of her men from day to day, that they may look into the endless years: *Qui autem docti fuerint, fulgebunt*,— "And they that be wise shall shine as the brightness of the firmament; and they that turn many to righteousness as the stars forever and ever" — *in perpetuas alternitates;* God's forever, man's forever.

Thoughts like these which have been presented were in the heart and in the mind of him whose name and life are now in our minds and hearts, and will long remain in this college which he loved so well. He meant that every student here should feel that she is to live forever, and should equip herself for the endless years. He knew that the study of truth in all its branches would be of enduring profit. He sought that by the personal knowledge of Him who is the truth, the student should fashion her purposes and construct her life. He would have the present the earnest of the future, and the future the fulfilment of the present. He taught the boundless need of the best ministries, and would have that spirit of helpfulness which seeks to confer an endless benefit. He would encourage fidelity by the vastness of its results. He would have it felt that to bring a soul into the obedience of Christ, to strengthen one in the Christian life, to promote piety and holy service, is to accomplish that which will abundantly repay all efforts and sacrifice, in that it will be an eternal good. He saw that it was an endless path which opens where you stand, and that if you will enter it, you shall find God walking with you among the lilies, and leading you where, at length, the stars will be gleaming about your feet.

He called this Christ's College. He would not have it bear his own name, nor let his face look down upon you from the walls. He meant that you should see the Lord. His last word to the teachers was, "Have faith: work and pray: be laborers together with God." His last word to the students was, "Work for one another, and try to lead souls to God. Place Christ first, in all things and always."

This is his benediction. They who receive it shall live by the power of an endless life.

Press-work by Rockwell & Churchill.

www.ingramcontent.com/pod-product-compliance
Lightning Source LLC
Chambersburg PA
CBHW022019240426
43667CB00042B/947